LOMELINO'S CAKES

LOMELINO'S CAKES

27 Pretty Cakes to Make Any Day Special

LINDA LOMELINO

Roost Books
Boston & London
2014

CONTENTS

CAKES

WHY CAKES?

Yes, why indeed only cakes? Perhaps it is because my mother—who was not necessarily a "supermom"—always made time to bake cookies and cakes when I was little. At our house, home baked ruled on weekends, unlike the bags of candy offered at my friends' homes. And, when we were at our grandmother's, we were always treated to a mountain of sweets! We started with cookies, continued with cake, and finished with ice cream. I have lots of fond memories of baked goods of all sorts.

Another type of pastry that I think about a lot and look forward to every year comes in the mail from my aunts in Portugal. The cake is baked in Madeira around Christmastime and called *bolo de mel*, which roughly translates as "honey cookie" or "honey cake" (although it doesn't have any real honey in it).

The idea that my blog, *Call me Cupcake!*, would feature recipes and photos of pastries was more or less a given. I have always loved both baking and photography. For me, fine pastry, and, most of all, a pretty cake, is a type of art form. Still, it was pure chance that I began the blog. Only in hindsight did I see how clear the path was!

It is so wonderful that I could combine baking with my other strong passion, photography, in my first book. Now I can share with you the cake recipes that I love the most. In this book, you'll also find information about the equipment you'll need and what ingredients you should focus on. In addition, I offer step-by-step instructions and guidance for baking, filling, icing, and decorating a pretty cake—everything you need for creating cakes as smoothly and easily as possible.

Linda Lomelino

EQUIPMENT

Even if you don't have all the equipment listed in this section, you can still bake wonderful cakes. However, one piece of equipment is particularly important to make cake baking easier: a good quality cake pan.

ELECTRIC HAND MIXER OR STAND MIXER

You can do quite well with a trusty old hand beater, but often an electric mixer is necessary. For example, egg whites will never achieve the same volume when they are beaten by hand; an electric beater creates lofty, beautiful results with ease.

BLENDER

A blender is an ideal tool for finely grinding nuts and making fruit purées. With an immersion blender, you can blend ingredients directly in the saucepan or bowl.

KITCHEN SCALE

This useful piece of equipment will allow you to divide batter evenly among several pans. Having a scale is not absolutely necessary, but if you don't have one, it can be difficult to pour the same amount of batter into each pan. The cake will taste just as good even if it doesn't have exactly the same size layers. It's really more about aesthetics. You can easily eyeball the amount or apportion the batter with a measuring cup. If you have a digital scale with a tare function, the scale subtracts the weight of the bowl or pan and shows only the weight of the contents.

MEASURING CUPS AND SPOONS

A set of measuring spoons usually includes a tablespoon, teaspoon, half teaspoon, and quarter teaspoon. When using these tools to measure amounts in a recipe, take a level, not rounded, amount. Level flour in a measuring cup by swiping your index finger or a butter knife straight across the top of the cup.

SPATULA

It's easier to get all the batter out of a mixing bowl with a rubber or silicone spatula.

BAKING PANS

All the cakes in this book were baked in light aluminum cake pans either 6 inches or 8 inches in diameter. Choose a pan about 3 inches high so the batter will have room to rise. Aluminum pans distribute the heat evenly during baking because they are thin.

You can also bake the 6-inch cakes in a larger baking pan or in a springform pan, about 7 to $9^{1}/_{2}$ inches in diameter. Keep in mind that the baking time may be shorter for a wider, shallower cake. Use a cake tester or skewer to determine if the cake is completely baked—the tester will come out with moist crumbs if the cake is done. And no two ovens bake alike, so always keep an eye on your cake while it's baking.

One large layer can be divided into three smaller layers. Freezer cakes are best made in a 7 to $9^{1}/_{2}$-inch diameter springform pan.

BAKING PARCHMENT PAPER

You can use baking parchment paper to line the pan if you think the cake will rise too high (see page 19). You can also lay parchment on the bottom of the pan and butter and flour the sides of the pan.

CAKE TURNTABLE

A footed, rotating cake stand or platter makes it easier to fill, cover, and decorate a cake.

OFFSET SPATULA

An offset or angled spatula is almost a necessity for covering a cake evenly. The difference is huge!

SMOOTHER

This tool is useful for covering a cake with fondant. By using a smoother, you'll achieve a smooth and attractive surface that will be even all around. Draw the smoother over the cake when it is "completely dressed" to smooth it out.

COOKIE CUTTERS AND MOLDS

Press these metal or plastic forms into the dough or fondant to form, for example, ginger cookie hearts or flowers.

PASTRY BAG AND TIPS

All kinds of styles and sizes of pastry bags are available, and what you choose depends on what type of decorations you want to make. You can find inexpensive plastic tips packaged with pastry bags in the grocery store. Better-quality tips are sold in most of the larger grocery stores, in specialty shops, or on the Internet.

A good rule of thumb is to begin with a couple of regular round tips, a large and a small, and a couple different star tips. I use the star tips most often because it is easy to vary the results when you pipe with them. Just a little imagination goes a long way!

Professional rustproof bakery tips can now be purchased on a number of Internet sites, and if you are lucky, your neighborhood has a well-stocked kitchen shop where you can find these items.

CAKE TESTER

If you stick the tester down through the center of the cake and it has moist crumbs when you pull it out, then the cake is done.

SKEWERS

You can also use skewers to test cake doneness. In addition, skewers are useful for making simple decorations such as flags and pennants and as supports when you assemble multilayer cakes (see page 28).

SUPPORTS FOR MULTILAYER CAKES

Use supports so the stacked layers don't sink down into each other when you are building a multilayer cake. You can find supports of various sorts depending on how large and high the cake is, then trim them to the desired length. Even a drinking straw can function as a support.

DOUBLE BOILER

When you need to heat or melt delicate ingredients that won't tolerate high, direct heat, such as eggs and chocolate, you can do it over a double boiler (also called a bain-marie or water bath).

Choose a heatproof bowl large enough to place over a saucepan. Fill the pan with water, but don't let the water come up to the bowl. Bring the water to a boil, and then let it simmer so that the steam from the water, rather than the water itself, heats the contents in the bowl.

RECOMMENDED INTERNET SHOPS

Paste coloring or natural food coloring, powdered color, tips, cookie cutters and molds, cake testers, and much more are available at the following Internet cake supply shops. No doubt an online search of your own will yield many other options.

US favorites:
www.williams-sonoma.com
www.joann.com
www.globalsugarart.com
www.cakeart.com

My favorites in Sweden:
www.kakburken.se
www.strosselannat.se
www.tartdecor.se
www.lyckasmedmat.se

INGREDIENTS

Good ingredients are the basis for baking good cakes, so simply put, buy the best ingredients you can afford. In particular, choose high-quality chocolate, organic eggs, and real butter instead of margarine.

EGGS

Most recipes are baked with large eggs (see the box below). Take the eggs out of the refrigerator 60 to 90 minutes before baking so they can come to room temperature. To speed up the process, you can place them in a bowl of warm water. However, if you are going to separate the whites from the yolks, you should do so when the eggs are still cold from the refrigerator; otherwise, the yolks can easily disintegrate.

Because egg yolks contain fat, it is important not to let any of the yolk mix with the white, as that prevents the whites from being beaten to stiff peaks. When you whisk the whites, it is also very important that the bowl is clean and free from any fats or oils. If you want to be completely sure, you can "butter" the bowl by adding a few drops of vinegar or lemon juice to a bit of paper towel, then wiping the interior of the bowl. It is best to whisk egg whites in a stainless steel or glass bowl, both of which are easier to clean than plastic bowls. The whites should be at room temperature in order to reach top volume.

When separating the whites and yolks of several eggs, have three small bowls ready. Crack an egg at the center, and let the egg white run out into one of the bowls. Lay the yolk in another bowl. When you crack open the second egg, let the white run into the third bowl and put the yolk in the second bowl with the first yolk. Now you can combine the second egg white with the first then continue the same way if you have several eggs to separate. This way, if something goes wrong and a yolk gets into a white, you won't have wasted all the egg whites.

BUTTER AND OIL

Use real butter when you bake, not margarine. Unless otherwise specified in the recipe, always let the butter come to room temperature; otherwise, the batter can separate when the butter is added to the other ingredients. If the butter is too cold, cut it into small cubes, place them on a plate, and let them sit in a warm place for a little while to soften.

When baking cakes, it is best to use salted butter so you don't have to add extra salt to the recipe. For buttercream and meringue buttercream, unsalted butter is best.

Butter is commonly packaged in 1-pound boxes with 4 sticks to the pound. In this book, we've used "stick" as our unit of measure for butter: 1 stick equals 8 tablespoons.

IF THE BATTER SEPARATES

After the butter and sugar have been beaten together, the batter can separate once the eggs are added. This happens when the ingredients aren't all at the same temperature.

The batter can usually be rescued when the flour mixture is added. If that doesn't work, try placing the bowl with the batter in a double boiler (see page 10) for a few minutes then whisk constantly until the batter becomes smooth.

If the batter doesn't cohere, you should bake the cake in any case—sometimes it will be perfectly fine, sometimes it simply won't rise as high as it should.

The same principle applies to frosting. If it separates, that usually means that the butter or soft cheese was too cold. Use the same double-boiler technique to smooth out the consistency.

HOW MUCH DO EGGS WEIGH?

Small egg	1½ oz.
Medium egg	1¾ oz.
Large egg	2 oz.
Extra large egg	2¼ oz.

If the recipe includes oil, choose a neutral-flavored oil, such as sunflower or canola, that won't affect the taste.

CHOCOLATE

Use the best chocolate you can afford (or the chocolate you like best!). If you wouldn't want to eat it, then you don't want to bake with it either. If you don't like the bitterness of dark chocolate, keep in mind that it will be blended with other ingredients when used for baking.

If you substitute milk chocolate for dark chocolate for baking, the chocolate taste will be much less distinct. Also consider that some recipes will need to be adjusted if you use milk or lighter chocolates instead. In a ganache (see page 54), you need less cream if you substitute milk chocolate for dark chocolate.

Chocolate can be melted in a microwave or in a double boiler on the stovetop at very low heat. Chocolate burns easily, and so you should melt it very carefully. White chocolate burns even more quickly than dark, so you need to be extra careful with it. Chocolate can burn and turn grainy in just a few seconds in the microwave, and there is no trick to rescuing it!

If you melt chocolate in a bowl over a double boiler, it is very important that you not let a single drop of water get near the bowl. It doesn't take much for the chocolate to be ruined. Remove the bowl from the heat when most of the chocolate has melted, and stir it a few times with a clean, dry utensil until it is totally melted.

FLOUR

I usually use white all-purpose flour when I bake, but you can choose any type you prefer. At home in Sweden, I like to bake with locally produced flour from Berte Mill in Slöinge. Choose a high-quality flour company that you trust, and always use the most wholesome, least processed flours they offer. (King Arthur and Bob's Red Mill are widely available in the United States and offer delicious results.)

When measuring flour, do not pack it too tightly into the measuring cup. First stir the flour in the bag to make it easier to measure. All of the measurements in the recipes are level. You can level the flour by swiping your index finger or a butter knife straight across the top of the cup.

When sifting flour, pour it into a fine sieve and let it pass through the sieve into the bowl. That removes any lumps that might be difficult to blend in, and the flour will be airy and distribute evenly. You can also pour the flour into a bowl and whisk it lightly with a hand whisk to aerate it.

SUGAR

Many people consider sugar nonnutritious and rather unnecessary, but in baking, sugar plays other roles besides sweetening: it adds texture and lightness, and preserves the cake.

GRANULATED SUGAR, or regular white sugar, is used for most of the recipes here.

CONFECTIONERS' SUGAR is finely sieved white granulated sugar that has been blended with cornstarch to prevent clumping. It is useful when you don't want the sugar crystals of regular sugar, as, for example, when you sprinkle powdered sugar over a cake or berries or when you use sugar in frosting or glazes.

BROWN SUGAR is white sugar that has been mixed with molasses for a golden brown, moist, and very flavorful sugar.

MUSCOVADO SUGAR is a type of raw sugar produced in Mauritania available in both light and dark varieties. The light tastes caramel-like, and the dark has a licorice flavor. Both types can be found in well-stocked grocery stores. If you can't find Muscovado sugar in your grocery, substitute brown sugar.

You can also experiment with CANE SUGAR, COCONUT SUGAR, and any other varieties you find at a natural grocer, if you'd like. Keep in mind that your results may vary from mine, though they will be just as delicious and pretty.

JAM SUGAR, also known as jelly sugar, is used with ingredients that need to set or gel. Called "gelling sugar" in Europe, it contains pectin and sometimes citric acid as a preservative.

FRUIT AND BERRIES

Use fresh berries (in season) and fruit, not frozen. A simple trick for finding the best citrus fruits (oranges, limes, and lemons are among the citrus fruits used in several recipes in this book) is to smell them. The peel should smell fresh and citrusy. Overripe bananas are perfect for baking—they taste much sweeter than unripe bananas!

COLORING

When coloring frosting and cake batter, you'll get the best results with the so-called paste dyes (also known as gel paste or gel food coloring). You only need a small amount of these thick and concentrated liquid colorings. Use a toothpick to drop the coloring in the bowl, and use a new toothpick if you need to add more color.

Colors also come in powder form, but you need to use much more of them to get the desired result. Powdered coloring and edible glitter work very well for painting fondant or flower paste decorations. With powdered coloring, you can paint shading or other nuances on, for example, a flower. The powdered coloring can also be mixed with a bit of neutral vodka for a more fluid color.

If you prefer a more natural approach, try one of the many brands of natural food coloring available, or you can experiment with puréed berries. Again, feel free to experiment, but your results may vary from mine.

FRESH OR SOFT CHEESE

Fresh or soft cheeses, such as cream cheese, are produced from cow's milk and have a fresh, tangy flavor that blends quite well into most baked goods because the acidity nicely balances the sweetness. A number of different brands and varieties are available.

Always choose the "natural" flavor of the original, full-fat version for CREAM CHEESE. Light versions don't lend the same creaminess.

MASCARPONE is an Italian soft cheese made from cow's milk and similar to cream cheese in many ways. It has a somewhat stronger flavor and slightly thicker consistency. Mascarpone is one of the ingredients in the classic Italian dessert tiramisù.

COTTAGE or CURD CHEESE is another type of fresh cheese that is commonly used in desserts and baking.

YOGURT is another tangy product most often made from cow's milk that is common in desserts and baking. Note that the texture and thickness of yogurt vary by brand and style; Greek yogurt is extra-thick and extra-tangy.

MILK

Use the milk you have on hand, preferably milk with at least 1.5 percent fat. Some recipes suggest whole milk (which has about 3.25% fat) for creamier results.

CREAM

Cream, unlike many other ingredients, should be refrigerator temperature when used for baking.

Use cream with a fat content of 36 to 40 percent when it will be whipped. Before you begin whipping the cream, chill the bowl and hand or electric beaters in the refrigerator or freezer for 10 minutes. The chilled equipment makes it easier to whip the cream, and the end result will be more stable. Begin whipping at low speed to prevent the cream from splashing out of the bowl. When the cream starts to thicken, beat at a higher speed, but keep an eye on it so it doesn't become too hard or grainy.

If you have whipped the cream too much, you can rescue it—as long as it hasn't turned to butter—by adding in one tablespoon of unwhipped cream at a time until it reaches the desired consistency. Don't whip it any more!

VANILLA

The aromatic flavor of vanilla goes well in most baking (and even in some main dishes). Slice down the entire length of the vanilla bean and scrape out the seeds with a knife. Often the vanilla bean is boiled with cream or milk to infuse it.

Pure vanilla can be bought as whole vanilla beans, vanilla powder, and extract. A bottle of vanilla powder contains vanilla bean in powder form. Vanilla extract is made from vanilla beans that have been soaked in alcohol. You can make homemade vanilla extract by soaking vanilla beans for a long time in the liquor you prefer: vodka, gin, even whiskey or bourbon (see the box on page 17).

Vanilla sugar is confectioners' sugar mixed with vanilla bean seeds and natural vanilla flavor from spruce wood (lignin).

The type of vanilla varies by where in the world it was grown. The most common types are bourbon (or bourbon Madagascar vanilla), Mexican, and Tahitian vanilla. Bourbon vanilla is the most common of the three. Tahitian vanilla is considered the most luxurious and is priced accordingly. Imitation vanilla extract may also be used as a more economical choice. Although liquid imitation vanilla is preferable, a powder version is also acceptable and is measured equally.

LICORICE

You can use licorice powder to flavor both cake layers and buttercream or frosting. Licorice powder is common in Sweden but may not be as prevalent around the world. It is made from raw licorice and can be found in specialty shops or on the Internet from chocolate shops or lakritsroten.se. It has a unique salty flavor. Liquid imitation licorice flavoring is a more economical option.

NUTS

Many types of nuts can be used in cake recipes, including almonds, hazelnuts, peanuts, cashews, Brazil nuts, walnuts, and so on. You can also buy nuts in various forms: shelled, unshelled, roasted, salted, smoked, candied, and pieces. All are delicious in baking, and many are easily substituted for each other in recipes. Eat what you love!

The skin of a nut is often rather bitter, so take the time to remove it (especially from hazelnuts and whole peanuts), even if doing so is messy and feels tedious. Your results will be tastier.

Toasting nuts and almonds intensifies the flavor and produces a good consistency. Toast nuts in the oven at 350°F to 400°F for 7 to 15 minutes, but keep an eye on the nuts because they can burn quickly. They are ready when they have taken on a light golden color and smell good.

Nuts contain a lot of nutritious fat, but the fat can go rancid rather quickly. Always store nuts in a cool place, preferably in the refrigerator. Nuts can also be stored in the freezer.

SUGAR AND FLOWER PASTE

FONDANT is a sugar paste similar to marzipan (or almond paste) in consistency, but it doesn't contain any nuts. Unlike marzipan, fondant is pure white. The consistency varies depending on the brand, so choose the paste from a company whose products you like. Fondant also comes in various flavors.

FLOWER PASTE (also called gum paste) is similar to fondant but it can be rolled out very thin. That quality makes it better for details such as flowers and ruffles. It hardens fairly quickly.

HOMEMADE VANILLA EXTRACT

Extract, which darkens over time, can be kept for several years. Top up the bottle or jar with more alcohol and vanilla beans as you use it up.

1 cup vodka (or gin, whiskey, or bourbon)
3 vanilla beans

1. Slice down through the length of each vanilla bean, and open the pod.
2. Place the beans in a glass bottle or jar, and pour in the vodka. Close the bottle or jar, and shake it well.
3. Leave the container in a cool, dark place for at least 2 months. Shake it every now and then.

HOMEMADE VANILLA SUGAR

When you scrape out the seeds from a vanilla bean, don't throw away the bean because a lot of flavor still remains there. Place the bean pod in a jar with some granulated sugar, and store it for 1 to 2 weeks. Stir it occasionally. Substitute the vanilla sugar for regular sugar when baking to add an extra taste of vanilla.

BAKING CAKE LAYERS

I'm often asked why I use such small cake pans. Well, it is because I like small cakes—they are so cute! It is quite rare that I need to bake a large cake. Usually I don't have more than 10 to 12 guests at a time, and a 6-inch diameter cake is enough to serve that many. Besides, wouldn't it be a shame to throw away leftover cake?

Another advantage to baking small cakes is that you can fit several 6-inch pans in the oven and avoid having to bake in several stages. It also takes less time to bake smaller cakes. Of course, you can bake in larger pans. Just remember that you need to adjust the baking time and that the finished cake will be shorter. If you still want to bake a high cake, you can double the recipe. (Don't forget to double the amount of filling, too!) You can buy smaller cake pans in well-stocked shops and from a number of Internet vendors.

In many of my recipes, I suggest that you bake the cake layers in several pans. The reason for that is quite simple: as the cakes rise, there is the risk that they will run over the top. It can also be difficult to bake the cake evenly if all the batter is baked in the same pan.

Certain kinds of cakes are better to bake in only one pan, for example, light and airy layers without butter (such as the Lemon Lover's Dream Cake, page 105, and the Cardamom Cake with Blueberries, page 58). For these cakes you can construct a collar for the pan with parchment paper so that the batter can rise up to the top edge. Certain cakes are still too "heavy" for the collar. You can always bake the cake layers in the same pan in several stages, but it will take much longer. If you do a lot of baking, it is worthwhile to invest in two or more pans.

If you want to use a baking pan or springform pan that is 7 to 9½ inches in diameter, you can divide the batter and bake in two stages—the baking time will be somewhat shorter because the layers are thinner—or bake all the batter at the same time and increase the baking time. Check the progress of the baking with a cake tester, which should come out with moist crumbs if the layer is ready. Often the cake won't rise as high when you bake the entire batter in the same pan.

For most of the recipes, all you have to do to prepare the pans is to butter them and sprinkle them with flour or bread crumbs through a small mesh strainer. To minimize the number of crumbs, flour is best. You can use parchment paper instead of buttering and flouring or breading the pan, but make sure that the collar meets the edge precisely so there is no spillover.

I always bake in a conventional oven with top and bottom heating elements. Bake the cakes in the center of the oven unless otherwise specified, and never open the oven door less than 20 minutes after beginning so that the layers don't collapse.

To test the layers for doneness, insert a cake tester or skewer into the center of the cake. If the tester comes out with moist crumbs, the cake is done.

Let the layers cool in their pans for at least 10 minutes before you unmold them (unless otherwise specified) so the layers don't fall apart. But don't wait too long because the extra heat from the pan will make the layers spongy. Turn the layers out onto a wire cooling rack that allows air to circulate all around the cake.

If you can't get the layers out of the cake pans, carefully run a knife or spatula all around the cake and all the way to the bottom of the pan. Carefully push the knife toward the layer to loosen it from the pan. Then, turn the pan upside down and gently tap it.

It is a good idea to bake the cake layers the day before the cake will be decorated. You can store the layers overnight in a plastic bag or put them in the freezer for about an hour. Cold layers are easier to divide and fill (see pages 21 and 22).

You can freeze all the cake layers, which is an excellent way to be prepared if you can't bake a cake the same day. Freeze each of the layers in a separate plastic freezer bag so they don't stick to each other and become difficult to separate.

YOU'LL NEED: baking parchment paper, baking pan, pencil, scissors, butter or oil

Place the cake pan on a piece of parchment paper. Trace the outline of the entire pan with the pencil.

Cut out a circle just inside the pencil line.

Measure how much paper will be needed for the collar. Cut it a bit higher than the baking pan.

Cut small notches along one of the long sides of the paper strip. Coat the inside of the pan with butter or oil.

Place the strip with the notches at the bottom of the pan and fold in the small flaps all around the bottom. The strip should overlap by 1¼–1½ inches (it should also be longer than the circumference of the baking pan on the inside). Use a little extra butter or oil to join the edges.

Lay the circle of parchment paper in the bottom of the pan so it fits snugly. Make sure that the collar isn't too high to fit in the oven. If it is, cut it down to the appropriate height.

DIVIDING A CAKE INTO SEVERAL LAYERS

Most cakes in this book are baked in two pans with each layer later divided in half horizontally. To make it easier to do this, let the cake layers rest for a few hours after baking or put them in the freezer for an hour (after they have cooled). Cold layers are easier to fill and frost because the cake will be less crumbly.

Use a serrated knife that matches the cake layer in size—the bigger the cake layer is, the bigger the knife should be. Rinse the knife in warm water and dry it between every cut. There are even special cake cutters (called *cake levelers*) that you can buy if it is too hard to divide the layers with a knife.

Keep in mind that it is easier to divide a smaller layer that has been baked in a 6-inch pan than a larger cake baked in a 9-inch pan.

YOU'LL NEED: Baking parchment, cutting board or cake turntable, serrated knife

Place the layer on a cutting board or cake turntable covered by a piece of parchment paper. The paper keeps the cake from sticking to the platter.

If the top is rounded, even it out with the knife.

Cut the layer horizontally at the center into two layers. Try to make them the same size. Cutting will be easier if you first mark the layer all the way around with a shallow cut before you cut through the whole piece.

STRAIGHT AND EVEN EDGES

Nice-looking cakes start with straight sides and flat tops. Those features also make decorating easier, quicker, and more fun! The trick for getting straight sides on a cake lies in how you stack the layers—especially the top layer: place it bottom up, the cut side down. That way the flat surface that was on the bottom of the baking pan will be facing up.

FILLING AND COVERING THE CAKE

With filling and covering materials such as frosting, you have the chance to "spackle" away any problems with the cake. Sometimes cake layers simply crumble. The best fix is a buttercream that firms up when chilled.

If the filling between the layers and the frosting that covers the cake aren't the same, make sure not to spread the filling too close to the edge as the next cake layer will press the filling even closer to the edge and may cause it to spill over. The end result is that the filling and covering will mix (which you don't want).

Please note that I tend to use a limited amount of frosting with my cakes to make sure that I have a good balance of flavors between the cake and the frosting. Your tastes may be different from mine, so if you want more frosting, increase the recipe by 50 percent or more.

FILL AND COVER WITH FROSTING

YOU'LL NEED: Cake turntable, cake board, cake plate, ice cream scoop, spatula

---

A SMOOTH AND PRETTY CAKE

If you want the buttercream or frosting to cover the cake evenly and smoothly, dip the offset spatula in warm water between each pass. Dry the spatula well before you continue.

Place the first layer on a thin cake board or cardboard or directly on a cake plate. Measure the filling with an ice cream scoop or something similar that you know will contain about the same amount of filling for each layer.

Spread the filling in an even layer using an offset spatula.

Stack the next layer, and repeat the above steps. Continue the same way, spreading the same amount of filling for each layer until you have used three of the layers.

Place the last layer on top, cut side down, to avoid crumbs on the cake surface and to ensure smooth, straight edges. Cover the cake with plastic wrap or a cake cover, and refrigerate it for a while.

Drop a relatively large amount of frosting on top of the cake and spread the frosting in an even layer across the top. Let any extra frosting hang over the edge, and then spread it down the side.

If necessary, add more frosting. The first thin layer of frosting keeps the crumbs in place and will smooth out any unevenness.

To ensure that the cake will have an even surface, refrigerate it again before you add the last layer of frosting. Chilling it will firm up the first layer of frosting.

Take the cake out of the refrigerator, and spread the next layer of frosting on the top of the cake. Continue down the sides all around the cake as before. Even out the sides and then the top of the cake by carefully drawing the offset spatula up and over the edge and in toward the center so that any extra frosting is pulled toward the center of the cake. Dry the spatula completely between each pass.

To make the sides of the cake smoother, you can run a dough scraper all the way around the cake. For a totally even and smooth surface, dip an offset spatula in warm water and dry it between each pass. When this is done, and you are satisfied with the cake, refrigerate it once more.

COVERING THE CAKE WITH FONDANT OR MARZIPAN

A fondant or marzipan cake can be prepared several days in advance. For example, you can bake the layers one day, fill the cake the next day, and cover and decorate it on day three. Fondant or flower paste decorations can be made several weeks in advance (see more about decorations on page 31).

Fondant cakes should be completely covered with buttercream, partly because the buttercream provides a stable and even base, and partly because the fondant won't be "melted" by the buttercream. Cream frostings placed under fondant have a tendency to "weep" and make the fondant too damp. If a cream frosting gets really damp, the fondant can begin to run. There is also a risk that any decorations with color will bleed and fade as well.

Fondant should be completely smooth and feel dry when handled to keep it as flexible as possible. It should be rolled out on a smooth and completely clean and dry surface (preferably a silicone rolling mat).

To determine the measurements for rolling out the fondant, measure the cake's height and diameter. If the cake is 4 inches high and 6 inches in diameter, calculate 4 + 4 + 6 + a little extra = 15–16 inches. That is how large the fondant should be. Count on using about 23–25 ounces of fondant for a 6-inch-diameter cake.

YOU'LL NEED: Fondant, cake board, rolling pin, rolling mat, confectioners' sugar to sprinkle on, measuring tape, smoother, knife or pizza wheel

When the buttercream layer has hardened, sprinkle a well-cleaned work surface with confectioners' sugar. Now knead the fondant or marzipan until it is soft and flexible. If you want to color it, use concentrated paste coloring so that it won't get wet. Begin by coloring a small amount and kneading it into the rest of the fondant. This prevents the color from getting too strong. It is better to start with only a little color because you can easily add too much if you aren't familiar with paste coloring.

Roll out the fondant as evenly as possible so that it is about ¼ inch thick (some recipes suggest an even thinner layer, but if you roll it out too thin, any unevenness in the cake will be more obvious). Sprinkle confectioners' sugar on the work surface to keep the fondant from sticking to the rolling surface. To ensure an even thickness and as an added precaution against sticking, rotate the piece as you roll it out.

Measure the diameter of the rolled-out fondant to be sure it isn't too big.

CLEAN HANDS

Always wash your hands thoroughly before you begin working with fondant. Dirt, dust, and food residue will show up instantly on the chalk white fondant.

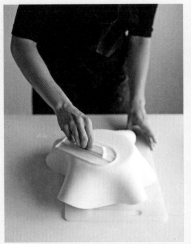

Lift the fondant, and place it on the cake. Support the fondant with your hands and forearms, or wind it into a rolling pin and unroll it onto the top of the cake. Try to center the fondant so that it hangs down evenly all around. Work carefully so you don't have to make adjustments; it isn't easy to shift the fondant once it is on the cake.

Begin by carefully smoothing the surface on the top of the cake with a smoother (see page 10) so the fondant stays in place.

Carefully smooth the fondant around the cake with your fingers and palms, beginning at the top and working down. Press carefully with your fingers to smooth out any blips.

Use a smoother to flatten the surface all around the cake. With the smoother, press down all around the base of the cake and score around the bottom edge. Now it will be easier to cut away any extra fondant.

Carefully cut away the excess fondant. Cut as close as possible to the edge without cutting away too much.

Smooth the surface of the fondant as much as possible. You might want to encircle the base of the cake with a silk ribbon. It should be cut slightly longer than the circumference of the cake and fastened with a little glaze (see page 28). A ribbon will also help to hide any cut marks.

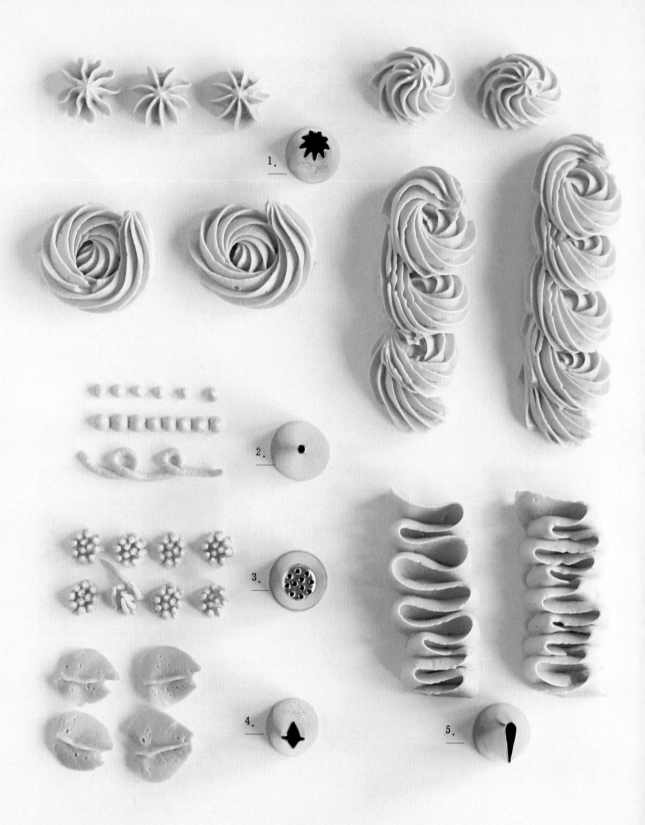

PIPING TECHNIQUES

By using a pastry bag and a few tips, you can add many fine details to your cake. Piping details all over the cake, takes quite a lot of frosting. If you don't want to make so much frosting, it's perfectly okay to pipe a few embellishments just on top of the cake.

TYPES OF TIPS

1. **STAR TIP.** A multisided and very useful tip available in many sizes and varieties. The little star tip in the photo is used for the Chocolate Cake with Blackberry Buttercream Frosting on page 62, the Orange and Dulce de Leche Cake on page 90, and the Lemon Lover's Dream Cake on page 105.

2. **ROUND TIP.** Good for making small details and beads around the cake (see the Strawberry Cake with White Chocolate on page 111).

3. **GRASS TIP.** Suitable for making fun decorations— for example, green grass on a children's cake.

4. **LEAF TIP.** Used only for piping leaves.

5. **RUFFLE TIP.** Good for piping out ruffles and various types of flowers (see the Peach Mousse Cake with Vanilla on page 118).

HIDING MISTAKES ON THE CAKE

You can hide any mistakes on the cake with a little extra frosting or decorations!

ASSEMBLING A LAYER CAKE

Cake layers can be stacked using one of several methods depending on how large or high the cake will be. A heavy cake with many layers may need cake supports or pillars in every layer except for the top one to prevent the layers from sinking into each other.

If it is a small layer cake that won't be moved, it isn't necessary to use pillars, but one support carefully stuck straight through the cake will make it more stable. If you want to make a heavy and high layer cake, it is a good idea to prepare each layer on a stable cake board exactly the same size as the cake. If you use cake boards between tiered layers, you can camouflage the cake board with fondant (the fondant will hang over the edge of the board).

This is the way many professional cake bakers prepare their layer cakes. If you are going to make a wedding cake in four layers, I recommend that you make the cake as stable as possible by preparing each layer directly on its own cake board and then assembling these.

STACKING THE LAYERS

1. Have two or more layers of different sizes ready. These can be covered with either frosting or fondant.
2. Begin with the bottom layer, which should be the largest layer, and place it on a cake plate or board (choose a sturdy model). Take a pillar, and insert it precisely in the center of the cake. Use a pen to mark the side of the pillar so it is $^1/_{16}$ inch taller than the cake itself. Carefully remove the support from the cake, and cut it precisely at the mark.

If the support is too short, the cake might collapse because the weight from the top layer will press down on the lower layer. If the support is too long, you risk having the top layer tip over.

A cake with more than two layers will need several pillars. Insert one support in the center of the cake and four around it an inch or so from the center. Measure to ensure that the placement of the supports is symmetrical.

3. Now mix the ingredients for the glaze (see the box below) and spread a thin layer over the center of the cake where the other layers will be placed. Carefully place the second layer exactly in the center. Measure if necessary. Let the glaze dry for a while before you decorate the cake.

HIDING CUT MARKS

Sometimes it is difficult to create perfectly even cut edges when slicing the various layers of a cake. If frosting, fondant, or decoration does not hide the rough cuts, wrap a silk ribbon around the base.

TEMPERATURE

Fondant can "weep" when the temperature changes, so you should take it out of the refrigerator a good while before you begin assembling the cake. The same rule applies when you are going to serve the cake.

ICING GLAZE

Icing glaze is a type of glaze made of egg white, confectioners' sugar, and usually a few drops of lemon. To assemble a layer cake, you don't need very much glaze, so blend a couple of tablespoons confectioners' sugar with a few drops of water at a time—it is easy to add too much water.

DECORATIONS

You can make a tasty and pretty cake with just a few tools. You're limited only by your imagination! One sure method is to decorate with fresh berries—that's always pretty, perfectly edible, and appreciated. Those who are a little more daring can try the tips below.

DECORATE MORE

Add colored frosting and/or decorations with the added flare of colored or chocolate sprinkles, chopped or melted chocolate, cocoa powder, or chocolate slivers (see page 93). Chopped or candied nuts or caramelized sugar are all decorative and tasty (see, for example, Nut and Nougat Fantasy on page 78, Orange and Dulce de Leche Cake on page 90, and Banana Cake with Caramel Frosting on page 95).

Fresh or fabric flowers are lovely decorations for a cake. Choose edible and unsprayed fresh flowers—ask your florist about which flowers to use. Alternatively, you can place flowers directly on the cake, with trimmed stems, or put a bit of florist tape on the back of the flower and stick the tape down into the cake so the flowers are held in place (see, for example, the Strawberry Cake with White Chocolate on page 111 and Peach Mousse Cake with Vanilla on page 118).

It is both fun and trendy to create your own decorations with skewers, paper, silk ribbon, or silk paper. Why not make your own small flags and pennants? Maybe a little flag or a heart to display the name of the birthday child? (See, for example, the Rainbow Cake on page 42 or the Red Velvet Cheesecake on page 115).

You can make any number of piped decorations with either whipped cream or frosting. Some piped shapes need a little more practice to get right, but a simple and quick way to make the cake pretty is to pipe rosettes of frosting on top of the cake with a star tip (see the Walnut and Coffee Cake on page 67 and the Lemon Lover's Dream cake on page 105). Use a spatula or spoon to make patterns or texture in the frosting (see the Chocolate and Espresso Cake on page 38 and the Rainbow Cake on page 42).

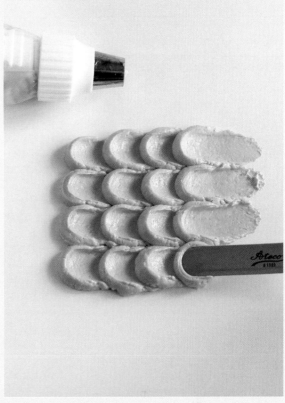

Dabs of buttercream or frosting can be shaped into a pretty pattern with an offset spatula.

Fondant, flower paste, or marzipan decorations make the cake especially pretty! That requires a few more materials and work, but the end result is well worth the effort (see the Frilly Cake on page 136).

MY BEST TIPS FOR MAKING
TASTY AND PRETTY CAKES

BEFORE YOU BEGIN: Prepare your work as much as possible before baking the cake. Clean off the work surfaces, get out any needed equipment, measure the ingredients, and so on. You'll save yourself a lot of cleaning up and chaos.

Use room-temperature ingredients (except for cream, which should be kept in the refrigerator). To speed up the process, place eggs in a bowl of lukewarm water; cut butter into small cubes, and warm milk in a saucepan on the stove.

To save time, prepare the frosting ahead and take out and measure the ingredients for the filling after baking, while the layers cool.

MIXING: When adding the flour mixture to the batter, do not beat too hard or too long because the cake could end up with a tough texture.

BAKING: If you want the cake layers to be as even as possible, weigh the batter on a kitchen scale and divide it evenly among the cake pans.

If the cake layers sink, it could be because the ingredients were too cold, the oven door was opened too soon, or the layers were taken from the oven too soon. If you started far enough ahead, you will still have time to bake more layers to replace those that were ruined! Don't forget that you can freeze cake layers and take them out to thaw when it's time to assemble the cake.

ASSEMBLING: To cut a finished cake cleanly, hold the knife under warm running water for 10 seconds, dry it off, and then make the cut. Do the same thing when you are cutting frozen cake layers.

The trick for getting a straight edge on a cake is to place the top layer bottom side up. That way the smooth, even surface that was on the bottom of the baking pan is facing up.

FROSTING AND DECORATING: Place the cake on a cake board to make it easy to work on. It can also then be moved or transported without any problems.

Start with a crumb coat of frosting. When it's time to cover the cake, begin with a thin layer of frosting all over the cake to catch any crumbs and hide any flaws, almost like spackling a wall. Put a little frosting at a time in a new bowl to avoid getting crumbs from the spatula in the main bowl of cake frosting. This step is especially important when you are making a colorful cake such as the Red Velvet Cheesecake (see page 115)—you don't want red smudges in a white frosting! Place the cake in the refrigerator for a while so the first layer can firm up a bit before the next layer is added.

STORING: All cakes can be stored, covered, in the refrigerator. Cream cakes should be removed from the refrigerator about 10 minutes before serving. Cakes with ganache, buttercream, or another type of frosting that has to set in the refrigerator should be taken out 30–60 minutes before serving. Keep in mind that cakes can absorb flavors from other foods in the refrigerator. Cakes covered with buttercream or fondant are often left out at room temperature and not refrigerated, but I don't recommend that.

Cake layers can be frozen for a couple of months. Even a finished cake can be frozen if it is well-protected. Cakes with buttercream are the best to freeze because they hold their consistency better than a cake made with a cream frosting. Here's another great freezer tip: slice the cake before you freeze it so you can thaw only the servings that you need when you want some!

SERVING: Cream cakes are best eaten the same day of baking, but, of course, the cake will also taste good the next day. Cakes with buttercream or another frosting are usually best after the layers have had time to set. For that reason, it's best to make the cake the day before the party. Cakes with meringue frosting are best eaten the same day.

CAKES

*Always read through the recipe from beginning to end
before you start baking so you will be well prepared!*

PAVLOVA

This meringue cake with chocolate, cream, raspberries, and pistachios is magnificently sticky and crispy. When the cake is finished, refrigerate it for a few minutes to make it easier to cut the layers. This cake should be made the same day it will be served.

8-10 SLICES

CHOCOLATE MERINGUE LAYERS
1³/₄ ounces dark chocolate
    (70% cocoa)
whites from 6 large eggs
1¹/₄ cups granulated sugar
3 tablespoons cocoa powder
1 tablespoon cornstarch
1 teaspoon white wine vinegar

**WHIPPED CREAM FROSTING
AND DECORATIONS**
1³/₄ cups whipping cream
1³/₄ ounces shelled pistachio nuts
    (about ¹/₂ cup)
8³/₄ ounces raspberries

MAKING THE CHOCOLATE MERINGUE LAYERS

1. Break the chocolate into small pieces, and melt them slowly over a double boiler (see page 10) or in the microwave. Let cool.
2. Preheat the oven to 350°F.
3. Cut a piece of parchment paper the size of your baking sheet. Then, cut out or find a circle template about 6 inches in diameter. Place the circles as far apart as possible on the parchment paper without touching the edges; trace. Turn the parchment paper over, and lay it on the baking sheet. These circles will indicate the placement of your meringue.
4. In a clean, dry bowl, beat the egg whites until soft peaks form. Add the sugar gradually, and continue beating to a thick meringue. You should be able to tip the bowl without the meringue sliding out.
5. Sift the cocoa powder and cornstarch into the meringue. Add the vinegar, and blend until the batter is smooth. Add the melted chocolate, and stir gently.
6. Divide the meringue among the paper circles. The meringues might shift during baking. Put the baking sheet into the oven, and lower the heat to 250°F.
7. Bake the meringue for 60–75 minutes. The baked layers should be hard and crisp around the edges but still sticky in the center. Turn off the oven, leaving the layers in the oven with the door propped open until the oven has cooled.

MAKING THE FROSTING AND DECORATIONS

1. In a dry, clean bowl, whip the cream until it thickens.
2. Chop the pistachios. Rinse and dry the raspberries.

ASSEMBLING THE CAKE

1. Place the first cake layer on a cake plate. Spread one-third of the Whipped Cream Frosting on the top, and sprinkle on a few raspberries. Repeat with the next layer. Place the third layer on top.
2. Top the cake with the remaining Whipped Cream Frosting, and then add the remaining raspberries and all the chopped pistachios.

CHOCOLATE AND ESPRESSO CAKE

Extra tall, extra chocolaty, extra everything! Chocolate cakes are unbelievably good and, when combined with a creamy chocolate and espresso frosting, will always be a hit. This cake is fluffy and moist.

8-10 SLICES

CHOCOLATE LAYERS
$^2/_3$ stick salted butter
$1^3/_4$ cups + 2 tablespoons flour
$^2/_3$ cup cocoa powder
$1^1/_2$ teaspoons baking powder
$1^1/_2$ teaspoons baking soda
$1^2/_3$ cups granulated sugar
2 medium eggs
$^1/_4$ cup + 2 tablespoons milk
$^2/_3$ cup strong, hot coffee or
    boiling water

**CHOCOLATE AND ESPRESSO
FROSTING**

*Using salted butter gives the
frosting an extra hint of salt!*

7 ounces dark chocolate
    (70% cocoa)
$2^1/_2$ sticks + 1 tablespoon salted
    butter, at room temperature
$1^1/_2$–$1^3/_4$ cups confectioners' sugar
$^2/_3$ cup cocoa powder
$^1/_2$ teaspoon vanilla powder or
    vanilla extract (or seeds
    from 1 vanilla bean)
4 tablespoons espresso or strong
    coffee (or 4 tablespoons
    whipping cream, for a milder
    flavor)

DECORATION
Chocolate sprinkles

MAKING THE CHOCOLATE LAYERS
1. Preheat the oven to 350°F.
2. Prepare two 6-inch cake pans with butter and flour, crumbs, or parchment paper (see page 18). Alternatively, prepare one pan and bake in two stages.
3. Melt the butter, and let it cool.
4. Sift the flour, cocoa powder, baking powder, and baking soda into a large bowl. Add the sugar, eggs, milk, and coffee, and beat for a couple of minutes until the batter is smooth.
5. Divide the batter evenly between the prepared pans.
6. Bake for 30–35 minutes.
7. Cool the layers in the pans for 15 minutes, and unmold them onto a wire cooling rack.

MAKING THE CHOCOLATE AND ESPRESSO FROSTING
1. Melt the chocolate in a double boiler (see page 10) or in the microwave. Set it aside, and let it cool to room temperature.
2. Beat the butter until light and creamy. Add the confectioners' sugar and cocoa powder a little at a time until evenly blended. Mix in the melted chocolate and vanilla.
3. Add the espresso, coffee, or whipping cream gradually, and beat for 2 minutes until the frosting is smooth and shiny.

Continued on page 41 ⇒→

SALTED OR UNSALTED?

When baking cakes, it is best to use salted butter so you don't have to add extra salt to the recipe. Some frostings, like Chocolate and Espresso Frosting, benefit from a hint of salt as well. For buttercream and meringue buttercream, unsalted butter is best.

ASSEMBLING THE CAKE

1. Slice each layer in half horizontally so you have four thin cake layers.
2. Place the first layer on a cake plate or cake board. Evenly spread the Chocolate and Espresso Frosting about $\frac{1}{4}$ inch thick over the cake layer. Repeat the process on the next two layers. Place the fourth layer on top, cut side down.
3. Spread a thin layer of Chocolate and Espresso Frosting all over the cake to contain the crumbs (see page 22). Refrigerate the cake for about 20 minutes or until the frosting has firmed up. You can leave the bowl of frosting out while the cake chills.
4. After the cake has chilled, spread the remaining frosting evenly around the cake.
5. Place the cake on a turntable. Rotate the platter while you hold a spatula or spoon (with the back of the spoon against the frosting), and carefully sculpt a pattern as shown in the photo on page 39. Begin at the side and finish with the top.
6. Decorate the cake with chocolate sprinkles.

RAINBOW CAKE

Appearances can be deceiving! Whoever cuts this cake will be pleasantly surprised when the pretty pink rainbow layers are revealed beneath the white, fluffy meringue exterior of the cake. The rainbow cake is easier to make than you might believe. Of course, you can choose your own favorite color for the cake layers if you don't like pink.

8–10 SLICES

RAINBOW CAKE LAYERS

1 stick + 1 tablespoon salted
    butter, at room temperature
1½ cups granulated sugar
2 teaspoons vanilla sugar
3¼ cups flour
1 tablespoon baking powder
1 cup whole milk
whites from 3 large eggs
pink paste coloring or natural
    food coloring

VANILLA SYRUP

¼ cup granulated sugar
¼ cup water
¼ teaspoon vanilla powder
    or vanilla extract

MERINGUE FROSTING

whites from 5 large eggs
1 cup granulated sugar
1 teaspoon vanilla sugar

MAKING THE RAINBOW LAYERS

1. Preheat the oven to 350°F.
2. Prepare five 6-inch cake pans with butter and flour, crumbs, or parchment paper (see page 18). Bake at most three pans at a time. Alternatively, prepare one pan and bake in several stages.
3. Beat the butter, sugar, and vanilla sugar until light and fluffy.
4. Blend the flour and baking powder in a bowl.
5. Alternate adding the flour mixture and the milk in several small amounts to the butter mixture. Beat everything to a smooth batter.
6. In a clean and dry bowl, whip the egg whites to stiff peaks.
7. Carefully fold the egg whites into the batter a little at a time. Divide the batter evenly among five bowls. Leave one bowl with plain batter, and color the rest in increasingly deep shades of pink (or your desired color).
8. Bake 25–30 minutes or until a toothpick inserted into the center comes out with moist crumbs.

MAKING THE VANILLA SYRUP

1. Blend the sugar, water, and vanilla in a saucepan.
2. Bring the mixture to a boil, and simmer for about 10 minutes. Let cool.

MAKING THE MERINGUE FROSTING

1. Pour the egg whites, sugar, and vanilla sugar into a heatproof bowl, and place it on top of a double boiler with water simmering in the lower pot. Beat constantly with a hand mixer until the temperature of the mixture reaches about 150°F on a candy thermometer or the sugar crystals have dissolved. Remove the bowl from the heat.

Continued on page 44 ⇒→

2. Beat the mixture with an electric hand mixer or stand mixer to a fluffy and white meringue. Continue beating until the meringue is cool and thick, which can take up to 10 minutes.

ASSEMBLING THE CAKE

1. Place the bottom layer on a cake platter or board. Begin with the uncolored or deepest color, whichever you prefer. Drizzle on some vanilla syrup, and then spread on a thin layer of Meringue Frosting. Repeat until you've used all the layers and they are stacked from lightest to darkest or vice versa.
2. Spread a thin layer of Meringue Frosting all around the cake to contain the crumbs (see page 22), and refrigerate it for 10–15 minutes.
3. Spread a thick coat of Meringue Frosting over the cake. Make the wave patterns by pressing into the frosting with an offset spatula or spoon.
4. Decorate the cake with one or more pennants made with skewers and pretty colored paper

CHOCOLATE AND LICORICE CAKE

You won't find a fluffier chocolate cake than this! Licorice and chocolate are an interesting and unexpected combination that I've totally fallen in love with. It only takes three teaspoons of licorice powder to give the cake a strong licorice flavor. If you prefer a milder taste, just use the lesser amount.

8–10 SLICES

CHOCOLATE LAYERS
3 large eggs
$1/3$ cup boiling water
6 tablespoons + 3 tablespoons
    granulated sugar, separated
$2^1/2$ tablespoons cocoa powder
$3/4$ cup flour
$1^1/2$ teaspoons cornstarch
$3/4$ teaspoon baking soda
pinch of salt
$1/4$ cup sunflower or canola oil
1 teaspoon vanilla sugar

**CHOCOLATE AND LICORICE
CREAM FILLING**
6 ounces dark chocolate
    (70% cocoa)
$2/3$ cup whipping cream
2–3 teaspoons licorice powder
$1^1/2$–2 tablespoons light corn
    syrup (or golden syrup)
$1/2$ stick unsalted butter

**CLASSIC VANILLA CREAM
FROSTING**
$2^1/2$ sticks + 1 tablespoon
    unsalted butter, at room
    temperature
$1^3/4$–$2^1/4$ cups confectioners' sugar
4–5 tablespoons whipping cream
1 tablespoon vanilla sugar
turquoise paste coloring
    (or natural food coloring)

DECORATION
white sprinkles (*nonpareils,*
optional)

MAKING THE CHOCOLATE LAYERS

1. Separate the egg whites and yolks into separate bowls (see page 12).
2. Preheat the oven to 325°F.
3. Bring the water to a boil, and let it cool.
4. Sift 6 tablespoons sugar, the cocoa powder, flour, cornstarch, baking soda, and salt into a mixing bowl.
5. Beat the oil, egg yolks, vanilla sugar, and water together. Sift in the dry ingredients, and beat only until the batter holds together. By sifting the dry ingredients twice, you'll be adding as much air as possible to the batter.
6. In a clean, dry bowl, beat the egg whites to soft peaks; slowly add the remaining 3 tablespoons sugar, 1 tablespoon at a time, and beat until the meringue is solid and thick. You should be able to tip the bowl without the meringue sliding out.
7. Carefully fold about one-fourth of the egg whites into the batter to lighten it. Fold in another quarter of the egg whites; repeat with the other two quarters. Do not mix more than necessary but just enough to eliminate any streaks of egg white.
8. Divide the batter evenly between two unbuttered, very clean 6-inch cake pans.
9. Bake the layers for about 30 minutes or until a toothpick inserted into the center comes out with moist crumbs.
10. As soon as you take the pans out of the oven, place them upside down on a wire cooling rack to prevent the cakes from sinking in the middle. The cooling rack allows air to flow all around the pans.
11. When the cake pans are completely cooled, carefully run a knife along the sides of each pan. Turn the pans upside down, and gently shake to loosen the layers.

Continued on page 48 ➡→

MAKING THE CHOCOLATE AND LICORICE CREAM FILLING

1. Chop the chocolate, and place it in a bowl.
2. Heat the cream, licorice powder, syrup, and butter in a saucepan until all the ingredients are melted and the mixture is heated through but not boiling.
3. Pour the warm mixture over the chocolate. Wait 30 seconds, and stir carefully until the cream is completely smooth and glossy.

MAKING THE CLASSIC VANILLA CREAM FROSTING

1. Beat the butter until light and fluffy, about 3–4 minutes.
2. Add the confectioners' sugar gradually, and beat to an evenly mixed batter. Add the cream and vanilla sugar.
3. Color the buttercream with paste coloring or natural food coloring (see page 15).

ASSEMBLING THE CAKE

1. Slice each layer in half horizontally so you will have four thin layers for the cake.
2. Place the first layer on a cake platter or board. Spread on an even layer of Chocolate and Licorice Cream Filling. Repeat until you have covered three layers. Place the last layer on top, cut side down.
3. Spread a thin layer of Classic Vanilla Cream Frosting over the whole cake. Refrigerate the assembled cake for about 20 minutes or until the layers have firmed up slightly.

PIPING ON THE ROSES

1. Fit a pastry bag with a small star tip, and fill it half full with Classic Vanilla Cream Frosting. Calculate the approximate number of roses you'll need for the height of the cake so you'll know how many to pipe out around the cake.
2. Begin at the bottom by piping out a circle around what will be the center of the rose. Try to form each rose in the same direction and end each at the same place. Continue all around the cake and work upward. Finish by piping out roses on top of the cake.
3. Optional: Decorate with small white sprinkles.

RASPBERRY BROWNIE CAKE

Meringue buttercream with fresh raspberries is the best frosting in my opinion! It tastes just as good as the best raspberry ice cream. If you prefer, substitute strawberries or blueberries for the raspberries—whatever is in season. Make sure that the cake is covered with the buttercream before you make the chocolate glaze so the glaze doesn't harden while you frost the cake.

8–10 PIECES

RASPBERRY BROWNIE CAKE
2 sticks salted butter
7 ounces dark chocolate
  (70% cocoa)
1 1/4 cups light Muscovado sugar,
  loosely packed in measuring
  cup
2/3 cup granulated sugar
4 large eggs
1 3/4 cups + 2 tablespoons flour
6 tablespoons cocoa powder
1 teaspoon baking powder
3 1/2 ounces raspberries, preferably fresh but frozen can be
  substituted

**MERINGUE CREAM WITH
RASPBERRIES**
whites from 4 large eggs
3/4 cup + 2 tablespoons
  granulated sugar
2 1/4 sticks unsalted butter,
  at room temperature
3 1/2 ounces raspberries
small amount pink paste coloring or natural food coloring
  (optional)

CHOCOLATE GLAZE
3 1/2 ounces dark chocolate
  (70% cocoa)
1/2 stick unsalted butter

DECORATION
Chocolate Glaze (see above)
raspberries

MAKING THE RASPBERRY BROWNIE CAKE
1. Preheat the oven to 350°F.
2. Prepare two 6-inch cake pans with butter and flour, crumbs, or parchment paper (see page 18). Alternatively, prepare one pan and bake in two stages.
3. Cut the butter into cubes, and coarsely chop the chocolate. Melt the butter and chocolate together at low heat in a large saucepan. Let cool.
4. Beat the Muscovado sugar, granulated sugar, and eggs until light and airy, about 3 minutes.
5. Mix the flour, cocoa powder, and baking powder in a separate bowl.
6. Pour the chocolate and butter mixture into the sugar and egg mixture, and beat to a smooth batter. Sift in the dry ingredients, and mix until the batter is smooth. Divide the batter evenly among the cake pans, and level the surface with a spoon. Divide the raspberries in half, and set one half aside. Press the other half of the raspberries into each layer.
7. Bake the layers for 45–50 minutes or until a toothpick inserted into the center comes out with moist crumbs.

MAKING THE MERINGUE CREAM WITH RASPBERRIES
1. Pour the egg whites and sugar into a heatproof bowl. Place it on top of a double boiler over a pot of simmering water. Whisk continually with a hand beater until the mixture reaches 150°F or the sugar crystals have dissolved. Remove the bowl from the heat.
2. Continue to beat the mixture with an electric beater or stand mixer until it is as white and fluffy as a meringue. Beat until the mixture is cool, which can take up to 10 minutes.
3. Add the butter a little at a time. After all the butter has been incorporated, beat for another 3–5 minutes.

Continued on next page ⟹→

4. Purée the remaining raspberries in a blender. Press the raspberry purée through a fine mesh to remove the seeds.
5. Mix the purée with the buttercream, and beat the frosting until it is smooth. For a stronger color, add some pink paste coloring or natural food coloring.

ASSEMBLING THE CAKE

1. Slice each layer in half horizontally so you have four thin layers for the cake.
2. Place the first layer on a cake plate or board. Spread on an even layer of Meringue Cream with Raspberries. Repeat for the next two layers. Place the last layer on top, cut side down.
3. Spread a thin layer of Meringue Cream with Raspberries all over the cake to contain the crumbs (see page 22). Refrigerate for about 20 minutes or until the frosting has firmed.
4. Add another layer of Meringue Cream with Raspberries until the cake is completely smooth. Place the cake in the refrigerator once more, and make the Chocolate Glaze while the cake chills.

MAKING THE CHOCOLATE GLAZE

1. Break the chocolate into pieces, and dice the butter.
2. Carefully melt the butter with the chocolate in a sauce-pan, and let it cool. The glaze will thicken somewhat but still be fluid.

DECORATION

1. Pour the Chocolate Glaze over the cake, and let it run down the sides. Use an offset spatula to spread the glaze more evenly if necessary. Work quickly before the glaze sets.
2. Decorate the cake with leftover raspberries.

BLACK FOREST CAKE

This is my version of the German Black Forest cherry cake, which you might think is a typical Black Forest cake, but it isn't. In my native Sweden, Black Forest cake consists of meringue layers, whipped cream, and grated chocolate. The German version of Black Forest cherry cake, which seems to have traveled farther and wider, has chocolate layers and cream with chocolate and cherries blended in—much like this cake.

8–10 SLICES

CHOCOLATE LAYERS
$^1/_4$ stick unsalted butter
$1^1/_4$ cups flour
6 tablespoons cocoa powder
1 teaspoon baking powder
1 teaspoon baking soda
pinch of salt
1 cup granulated sugar
1 large egg
$^2/_3$ cup milk
6 tablespoons boiling water

DARK CHOCOLATE GANACHE
$1^3/_4$ ounces dark chocolate
    (70% cocoa)
$^1/_4$ cup whipping cream

MASCARPONE FROSTING
8 ounces mascarpone cheese
$^3/_4$–1 cup confectioners' sugar
$1^1/_4$ cups whipping cream

FILLING
$3^1/_2$ ounces cherries soaked in
    rum (about $^1/_2$ jar)

DECORATION
fresh cherries
about 1 ounce dark chocolate,
    melted and cooled

MAKING THE CHOCOLATE LAYERS
1. Preheat the oven to 350°F.
2. Prepare two 6-inch cake pans with butter and flour, crumbs, or parchment paper (see page 18). Alternatively, prepare one pan and bake in two stages.
3. Melt the butter, and let it cool.
4. Sift the flour, cocoa powder, baking powder, and baking soda into a large bowl. Add the salt, sugar, egg, milk, and water, and beat for a couple minutes until the batter is smooth. Divide the batter evenly between the prepared pans.
5. Bake the layers for 25–30 minutes or until a toothpick inserted into the center comes out with moist crumbs.

MAKING THE DARK CHOCOLATE GANACHE
1. Chop the chocolate, and put it in a bowl.
2. Carefully heat the cream in a saucepan until it reaches the boiling point. Pour the cream over the chocolate, and let it stand a few minutes while you mix carefully. Blend the ingredients to a smooth and glossy chocolate cream. Allow the ganache to rest at room temperature until it is firm enough to spread on the cake.

MAKING THE MASCARPONE FROSTING
1. Mix the mascarpone and confectioners' sugar in a bowl.
2. In a separate bowl, whip the cream to stiff peaks. Then, fold in the mascarpone blend.

ASSEMBLING THE CAKE
1. Slice each layer in half horizontally so you have four thin layers for the cake.
2. Place the first layer on a cake plate or board. Begin by spreading an even layer of Dark Chocolate Ganache over the cake, and top it with one-third of the

Continued on page 56 ➠→

preserved cherries. On the bottom of the next layer, spread a thin layer of Mascarpone Frosting. Place the layers together so you have a "sandwich" of cake, ganache, cherries, mascarpone, and cake. Repeat until you've used all of the layers, making sure to place the last layer on top, cut side down.

3. Cover the entire cake with a thin layer of Mascarpone Frosting to contain the crumbs (see page 22). Refrigerate the cake for about 20 minutes or until the frosting has firmed slightly.

4. Spread the rest of the frosting over the cake in a smooth layer.

5. Pour the melted and cooled dark chocolate around the top of the cake so it runs over the edge a little. Decorate with fresh cherries.

VARIATIONS

If you don't like cherries soaked in rum, you can substitute fresh pitted cherries. Of course, you can also substitute any berries you like.

Mascarpone cheese can be substituted with cream cheese or another fresh cheese, but the frosting will have a runnier consistency.

CARDAMOM CAKE WITH BLUEBERRIES

Here's a very light cardamom cake baked without any oil or butter. If you don't have the time or inclination to make blueberry jam, you can, of course, use a store-bought variety. I promise, though, that the cake will be extra tasty with the homemade jam!

8–10 SLICES

CARDAMOM LAYERS

3 large eggs
1¼ cups granulated sugar
6 tablespoons milk
½ teaspoon vanilla powder
    or vanilla extract
1¼ cups flour
2 teaspoons baking powder
1 teaspoon freshly ground
    cardamom

**BLUEBERRY JAM WITH
VANILLA FILLING**

about 1 quart blueberries (just
    over 1 pound), very fresh
¾ cup jam sugar
6 tablespoons granulated sugar
1 vanilla bean

YOGURT FROSTING

1¾ cups whipping cream
¾ cup Turkish or Greek yogurt
    (10% milk fat)
2 tablespoons granulated sugar,
    or to taste

DECORATION

4½ ounces fresh blueberries

MAKING THE CARDAMOM CAKE

1. Preheat the oven to 350°F.
2. Prepare one 6-inch cake pan with a collar made from baking parchment. It should be at least 2 inches taller than the edge of the pan (see page 19).
3. Beat the eggs and sugar until light and airy, about 5 minutes.
4. Heat the milk with the vanilla, and add it to the egg mixture.
5. Mix the flour, baking powder, and cardamom in a separate bowl. Sift the dry ingredients into the batter, and carefully fold them in until the batter is well blended and free of lumps. Pour the batter into the prepared cake pan.
6. Bake for about 50 minutes or until a toothpick inserted into the center comes out with moist crumbs.

MAKING THE BLUEBERRY JAM WITH VANILLA FILLING

Make sure the jars are sterile before filling them with homemade jam. The easiest way to do this is to place the jars in the oven at 212°F for a few minutes. Jam sugar makes the jam the correct thickness, which is important when it will be used for cake filling.

1. Pour the blueberries, jam sugar, and granulated sugar into a large saucepan.
2. Cut the vanilla bean lengthwise, scrape the seeds out into the pan, and add the bean. Carefully bring the mixture to a boil while stirring constantly, and let it simmer at low heat for 10–15 minutes.
3. Skim any foam from the jam, and remove the vanilla bean. Pour the jam into a warm and sterile glass jar; seal. Store the jar in the refrigerator.
4. Reserve ½–¾ cup for the cake.

Continued on page 60 ⇒→

MAKING THE YOGURT FROSTING

1. Blend the cream, yogurt, and sugar in the bowl of a stand mixer.
2. Beat the mixture to stiff peaks.

ASSEMBLING THE CAKE

1. Slice the cake horizontally into three layers. Place the first layer on a cake plate or board. Cover the layer with an even coat of Blueberry Jam with Vanilla Filling; then spread on a thick layer of Yogurt Frosting. Repeat for a second layer. Place the last layer on the top, cut side down.
2. Cover the cake with a thick layer of Yogurt Frosting. Make a striped pattern in the frosting using an offset spatula or the back of a spoon, beginning at the bottom and working straight up (see the photo at right).
3. Decorate the top of the cake with blueberries and perhaps a little pennant made with a skewer and some pretty paper.

TIPS AND VARIATIONS

Blueberries and cardamom are a wonderful flavor combination, but if you don't like cardamom or simply want to vary the blueberry cake, you can use vanilla powder or vanilla extract instead.

The cardamom flavor will be much more distinct if you grind it with a mortar and pestle or crush the whole seed instead of using preground cardamom.

Make sure the blueberries for the top of the cake are dry and fresh, or the color will quickly bleed into the frosting.

The cake will look best if you use blueberries of the same size on the top or place the largest ones all around the edge and the smaller ones in the center of the cake.

CHOCOLATE CAKE WITH BLACKBERRY BUTTERCREAM FROSTING

This delectable cake tempts with moist chocolate layers and meringue buttercream flavored with fresh blackberries. If you want extra flavor, spread a little blackberry jam between the layers. If you don't like blackberries, use whatever berries you prefer, or what's in season. The amounts for the frosting are for a cake with piped decorations. If you want a smooth frosting, you can cut the recipe in half.

8–10 SLICES

CHOCOLATE LAYERS
1^1/$_2$ cups flour
1 teaspoon baking powder
^{1}/$_2$ teaspoon baking soda
3 tablespoons cocoa powder
^{2}/$_3$ cup sour cream
1^1/$_4$ sticks salted butter,
    at room temperature
^{2}/$_3$ cup granulated sugar
^{1}/$_4$ cup light Muscovado sugar
2 teaspoons vanilla extract
    or vanilla powder
2 large eggs

BLACKBERRY BUTTERCREAM FROSTING
whites from 8 large eggs
2 cups granulated sugar
4 sticks unsalted butter,
    at room temperature
7 ounces blackberries

DECORATION
white sprinkles (*nonpareils*)

MAKING THE CHOCOLATE LAYERS
1. Preheat the oven to 350°F.
2. Prepare two 6-inch cake pans with butter and flour, crumbs, or parchment paper (see page 18). Alternatively, prepare one pan and bake in two stages.
3. Mix the flour, baking powder, and baking soda in a bowl, and set it aside. Blend the cocoa powder with the sour cream, and set it aside.
4. In a separate bowl, mix the butter, granulated sugar, Muscovado sugar, and vanilla, and beat until light and fluffy. Add the eggs one at a time, and continue beating for a few minutes.
5. Alternate adding the flour mixture and the sour cream mixture in small amounts at a time, and beat for a couple minutes. Divide the batter evenly between the prepared pans.
6. Bake the layers for about 35 minutes or until a toothpick inserted into the center comes out with moist crumbs.

MAKING THE BLACKBERRY BUTTERCREAM FROSTING
1. Pour the egg whites and sugar into a heatproof bowl, and place the bowl on top of a saucepan of simmering water. Whisk constantly using a hand beater until the mixture is about 150°F or the sugar crystals have dissolved. Remove the bowl from the heat.
2. Using an electric hand mixer or stand mixer, beat the mixture until it is as fluffy and white as a meringue. Continue beating until the mixture has cooled, which can take up to 10 minutes.
3. Add the butter a little at a time. After all the butter has been incorporated, beat for another 3–5 minutes. (If your buttercream separates, see page 52.)

Continued on page 65 ➡→

4. Purée the blackberries in a blender. Press the berries through a fine mesh to remove the seeds.
5. Mix the purée with the buttercream, and beat until the frosting is smooth.

ASSEMBLING THE CAKE

1. Slice each layer in half horizontally so you will have four thin layers for the cake.
2. Place the first layer on a cake plate or board. Spread an even coating of Blackberry Buttercream Frosting over the layer. Repeat for the next two layers. Place the fourth layer on top, cut side down.
3. Cover the entire cake with a thin layer of Blackberry Buttercream Frosting. Refrigerate the cake for about 20 minutes or until the frosting has firmed slightly.
4. Fit a pastry bag with a small star tip, and fill the bag no more than two-thirds full of frosting. Beginning at the base of the cake, pipe out a shape that looks like the number 9, starting at the bottom of the number. Pipe "nines" in columns around the cake, working throughout in a continually sweeping motion.
5. Decorate with white sprinkles.

WALNUT AND COFFEE CAKE

This dessert is a real "grown-up" cake with a strong coffee flavor that will be a hit even with those who aren't very fond of coffee—I know this from experience. The Kahlúa (a Mexican coffee liqueur) can be omitted if you want a less "adult" taste.

12–15 SLICES

COFFEE AND WALNUT LAYERS
2³/₄ ounces (¹/₃ cup) walnuts
1¹/₂ tablespoons instant coffee
    powder
3 tablespoons hot water
2 sticks salted butter,
    at room temperature
³/₄ cup granulated sugar
4 large eggs
1¹/₃ cups flour
2¹/₂ teaspoons baking powder
¹/₂ teaspoon baking soda
2 tablespoons Kahlúa to sprinkle
    over the cake

COFFEE AND LIQUEUR FROSTING
2 tablespoons instant coffee
    powder
1 tablespoon hot water
2¹/₂ sticks + 1 tablespoon
    unsalted butter, at room
    temperature
1¹/₄–1¹/₂ cups confectioners' sugar
3–4 tablespoons whipping cream
2–3 tablespoons Kahlúa (optional)

DARK CHOCOLATE GANACHE
1³/₄ ounces dark chocolate
    (70% cocoa)
¹/₄ cup whipping cream

DECORATION
chocolate malt balls
chocolate sprinkles

MAKING THE COFFEE AND WALNUT LAYERS

1. Preheat the oven to 350°F.
2. Prepare two 8-inch cake pans with butter and flour, crumbs, or parchment paper (see page 18). Alternatively, prepare one pan and bake in two stages.
3. Toast the walnuts in the oven until lightly browned, for about 5–8 minutes. When the nuts have cooled, finely grind them in a blender. Set aside.
4. Dissolve the instant coffee powder in the hot water. Set aside.
5. Beat the butter and sugar until light and fluffy, about 3–4 minutes. Add the eggs, one at a time, making sure each is incorporated before adding the next egg.
6. Mix the flour, baking powder, and baking soda in a separate bowl. Pour the dry ingredients and the ground walnuts into the egg mixture, and stir in the coffee. Beat until the batter is smooth. Divide the batter evenly between the prepared pans.
7. Bake the layers for about 25 minutes or until a toothpick inserted into the center comes out with moist crumbs.
8. Cool the layers in the pans for 10 minutes, and unmold the layers onto a wire cooling rack.

MAKING THE COFFEE AND LIQUEUR FROSTING

1. Dissolve the instant coffee powder into the hot water, and let it cool.
2. Using an electric mixer, beat the butter until it is white, then blend in the confectioners' sugar, coffee, cream, and, finally, the Kahlúa. Continue beating until the frosting is smooth and fluffy.

MAKING THE DARK CHOCOLATE GANACHE

1. Chop the chocolate, and put it in a bowl.
2. Heat the cream in a saucepan until it reaches the boiling point.

Continued on next page ➡→

3. Pour the cream over the chocolate, wait 30 seconds, and stir until creamy and shiny. Let it cool until the ganache is firm enough to pipe.

ASSEMBLING THE CAKE

1. Slice each layer in half horizontally so you will have four thin layers for the cake.
2. Place the first layer on a cake plate or board. Sprinkle on some Kahlúa if you want an extra strong liqueur flavor.
3. Spread a thin coat of Coffee and Liqueur Frosting over the layer. Place the next layer on top, and cover it with a thin coat of Coffee and Liqueur Frosting. Continue until you've used three of the layers. Place the last layer on top, cut side down.
4. Spread a thin coat of frosting all around the cake. Refrigerate the cake for about 20 minutes until the frosting has set.
5. Spread on the rest of the Coffee and Liqueur Frosting in an even layer.
6. Spoon Dark Chocolate Ganache into a pastry bag fitted with a large star tip. Pipe ganache rosettes all around the top of the cake.
7. Top each rosette with a chocolate malt ball, and decorate the base of the cake with chocolate sprinkles.

MAPLE SYRUP CAKE

When shopping for maple syrup, don't let yourself be deceived by "pancake syrup." Make sure "100% pure maple syrup" is clearly printed on the label. And don't underestimate the effect of fresh flowers!

8–10 SLICES

MAPLE SYRUP LAYERS
³/₄ cup pecans (or walnuts)
³/₄ stick unsalted butter, at room
    temperature, plus more for
    buttering pans
¹/₂ cup light Muscovado sugar,
    loosely packed in measuring
    cup
6 tablespoons maple syrup
2 medium eggs
1¹/₄ cups flour
2 teaspoons baking powder
¹/₂ teaspoon ground cinnamon
¹/₄ teaspoon salt
³/₄ cup milk

MAPLE SYRUP FROSTING
(YIELDS ABOUT 2 CUPS)
whites from 3 large eggs
6 tablespoons granulated sugar
¹/₄ cup light brown sugar,
    not packed
4 tablespoons maple syrup
1¹/₂ sticks unsalted butter,
    at room temperature

DECORATION
fresh flowers, such as roses

MAKING THE MAPLE SYRUP LAYERS

1. Preheat the oven to 350°F.
2. Line three 6-inch cake pans with baking parchment (see page 19). Alternatively, line one pan and bake in several stages.
3. Toast the pecans in the oven for about 8 minutes. Let cool.
4. Beat the butter and Muscovado sugar until fluffy, about 3 minutes. Add the maple syrup, and beat to a smooth batter. Add the eggs one at a time, completely incorporating each egg before adding the next.
5. Sift the flour, baking powder, cinnamon, and salt into a bowl. Finely chop the nuts, and stir them into the flour mixture. Pour the dry ingredients into the egg mixture, and stir them in carefully. Add the milk, and beat to a smooth batter. Divide the batter evenly among the prepared pans.
6. Bake for 20–25 minutes or until a toothpick inserted into the center comes out with moist crumbs.
7. Cool the layers in the pans for 10 minutes, and unmold them onto a wire cooling rack.

MAKING THE MAPLE SYRUP FROSTING

1. Pour the egg whites and sugars into a heatproof bowl, and set it on top of a saucepan of simmering water. Use a hand whisk to beat the mixture continually until it reaches 150°F or the sugar crystals have dissolved. Remove the bowl from the heat. Add the maple syrup.
2. Beat the mixture with a hand or stand mixer until it is a fluffy meringue. Continue beating until the mixture is cool and thick (the meringue shouldn't slide out when you tilt the bowl). This can take up to 5 minutes or longer.
3. Add the butter a small amount at a time. Beat the frosting for 3–5 minutes after all the butter has been added. (If your buttercream separates, see page 52.)

Continued on next page ⇒→

ASSEMBLING THE CAKE

1. Place the first layer on a cake plate or board.
2. Spoon Maple Syrup Frosting into a pastry bag fitted with a large star tip. Pipe circles around the top, beginning at the outer edge and working in. It's easier to see what you are doing if you start at the outer edge. If you want the cake to be higher, pipe an extra circle around the outer edge, on top of the previous circle of frosting.
3. Place the next layer on top and pipe circles around it as for the first layer.
4. Place the last layer on top, cut side down. Leave the exterior of the cake unfrosted.
5. Decorate the cake top with fresh flowers (see page 31).

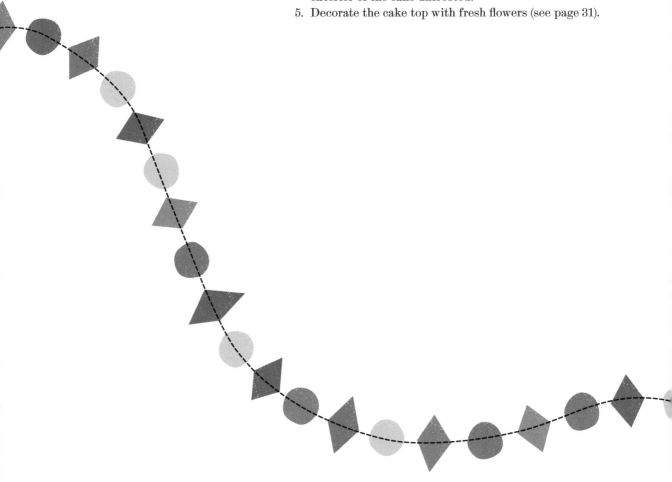

COOKIES 'N' CREAM

I've smuggled my favorite cookies into this eye-popping cake. These popular American chocolate cookies give the cake a great consistency—so it's just like a giant chocolate sandwich cookie. The pretty dark chocolate outside contrasts nicely with the inside.

8–10 SLICES

COOKIE-AND-VANILLA LAYERS
1/2 stick salted butter,
    at room temperature
3/4 cup granulated sugar
1/2 cup milk
1 teaspoon vanilla extract
    or vanilla powder
1 cup flour
1/2 teaspoon baking powder
1 large egg white
8 regular-size chocolate
    sandwich cookies

CHOCOLATE LAYER
1/4 stick salted butter,
    at room temperature
2/3 cup flour
1/4 cup cocoa powder
1/2 teaspoon baking powder
1/2 teaspoon baking soda
1/2 cup granulated sugar
1 medium egg
1/3 cup milk
1/4 cup boiling water

COOKIES AND CREAM CHEESE FROSTING
10 1/2 ounces cream cheese
3/4 cup confectioners' sugar
1 1/4 cups whipping cream
6 regular-size chocolate
    sandwich cookies

DECORATION
10–12 regular size chocolate sandwich cookies
10–12 mini chocolate sandwich cookies
1 cherry

MAKING THE COOKIE-AND-VANILLA LAYERS
1. Preheat the oven to 350°F.
2. Prepare two 6-inch cake pans with butter and flour, crumbs, or parchment paper (see page 18). Alternatively, prepare one pan and bake in two stages.
3. Beat the butter and sugar until fluffy, about 3 minutes.
4. Add the milk and vanilla extract, and beat to a smooth batter.
5. In a separate bowl, mix the flour and baking powder, then stir them into the batter. Add the egg white, and beat for another 2 minutes. Coarsely crush the cookies, and fold them in. Divide the batter evenly between the prepared pans.
6. Bake the layers for about 25 minutes or until a toothpick inserted into the center comes out with moist crumbs.
7. Cool the layers in the pans for 10 minutes, and unmold them onto a wire cooling rack.

MAKING THE CHOCOLATE LAYER
1. Preheat the oven to 350°F.
2. Prepare one 6-inch cake pan with butter and flour, crumbs, or parchment paper (see page 18).
3. Melt the butter, and let it cool.
4. Sift the flour, cocoa powder, baking powder, and baking soda into a large bowl. Add the sugar, egg, milk, and boiling water, and beat for a couple minutes until the batter is smooth. Pour the batter into the prepared pan.
5. Bake for about 30 minutes or until a toothpick inserted into the center comes out with moist crumbs.

Continued on next page ⟫→

6. Cool the layer in the pan for 10 minutes, and unmold it onto a wire cooling rack.

MAKING THE COOKIES AND CREAM CHEESE FROSTING
1. Mix the cream cheese and confectioners' sugar in a bowl.
2. In a separate bowl, whip the cream until it reaches the desired thickness, with soft peaks. Fold it into the cheese mixture.
3. Crush the chocolate sandwich cookies, and mix them with about one-third of the filling; this amount will be used to fill the cake. Use the remaining two-thirds of the frosting to cover the cake. If the frosting doesn't feel firm enough, refrigerate it for a short while.

ASSEMBLING THE CAKE
1. Place a cookie-and-vanilla layer on a cake plate, bottom side up. Spread half of the filling with cookie pieces on the top.
2. Put the chocolate layer on top, and spread the rest of the filling on it. Add the other vanilla layer, bottom side up.
3. Evenly spread the remaining two-thirds of the frosting (without the cookies) over the cake.

DECORATION
1. Grind the regular-size cookies in a blender.
2. Cover the top and the sides of the cake with cookie crumbs. Covering the sides will take a little time to produce an even coating, so work patiently. Use your palm to press the crumbs onto the cake. When you are satisfied, finish by carefully pressing all around the cake with a smoother (see page 10).
3. Decorate the cake with a few mini sandwich cookies and a cherry.

CHANGE THE COOKIES

Instead of sandwich cookies, use some other favorite cookies!

NUT AND NOUGAT FANTASY

Homemade nougat cream tastes much better than the store-bought variety, and it doesn't have a single additive. The cream is firm but spreadable and keeps in the refrigerator for about a week. It's a good idea to make it a few days ahead. If you want a softer cream, add a little more milk or omit the powdered milk, or use more milk chocolate and less dark chocolate.

8–10 SLICES

NOUGAT CREAM
3$^{1}/_{2}$ ounces hazelnuts
3$^{1}/_{2}$ ounces dark chocolate
    (70% cocoa)
1$^{3}/_{4}$ ounces milk chocolate
    (30% cocoa)
$^{2}/_{3}$ cup whole milk
$^{1}/_{3}$ cup powdered milk (optional)
1 tablespoon honey
pinch of salt
1$^{1}/_{4}$ cups whipping cream

HAZELNUT AND CHOCOLATE LAYERS
6 ounces hazelnuts
1$^{1}/_{2}$ sticks salted butter
whites from 6 large eggs
1 cup flour
$^{3}/_{8}$ cup cocoa powder
1$^{1}/_{4}$ cups confectioners' sugar
$^{1}/_{4}$ cup light Muscovado sugar,
    firmly packed in measuring
    cup

CANDIED HAZELNUTS
1$^{3}/_{4}$ cups hazelnuts
$^{1}/_{4}$ cup granulated sugar

CHOCOLATE FROSTING
5$^{1}/_{4}$ ounces dark chocolate
    (70% cocoa)
1$^{3}/_{4}$ sticks unsalted butter,
    at room temperature
1$^{1}/_{4}$ cups confectioners' sugar

$^{2}/_{3}$ cup cocoa powder
$^{1}/_{2}$ teaspoon vanilla powder or vanilla
    extract
3–4 tablespoons strong coffee

DECORATION
Make the same day as the cake will be served—preferably immediately before serving, so the caramel doesn't melt.

5–10 hazelnuts
6 tablespoons sugar

MAKING THE NOUGAT CREAM

Note: You can save yourself a step by toasting all of the hazelnuts for the Nougat Cream, the Hazelnut and Chocolate Layers, and the Candied Hazelnuts at the same time.

1. Preheat the oven to 350°F.
2. Toast the hazelnuts on a pan in the oven for 12–15 minutes. Watch them carefully as they can burn quickly. If they aren't already skinned, rub them in a hand towel, loosening as much of the skin as possible.
3. Grind the nuts in the blender until they are as finely ground as possible.
4. Melt the dark and milk chocolate in the top of a double boiler (see page 10) or in the microwave. Stir the ground nuts into the chocolate, and blend the mixture to a smooth cream.
5. Bring the milk to a boil, and add the powdered milk, honey, and salt. Cool the liquid for a few minutes, and

Continued on page 80 ⟩→

pour it over the chocolate mixture. Stir until the cream is smooth. Pour the liquid into a clean jar, and place it in the refrigerator.

6. While the cakes are baking, whip the cream in a separate bowl until it is quite firm, then blend in 1¼ cups of the chilled nougat, and beat until smooth.

MAKING THE HAZELNUT AND CHOCOLATE LAYERS

1. Preheat the oven to 350°F.
2. Toast the hazelnuts on a pan in the oven for 12–15 minutes. Watch them carefully as they can burn quickly. If they aren't already skinned, rub them in a hand towel, loosening as much of the skin as possible. Cool the nuts, and then finely grind them in a blender.
3. Prepare two 6-inch cake pans with butter and flour, crumbs, or parchment paper (see page 18). Alternatively, prepare one pan and bake in two stages.
4. Melt the butter, and set it aside to cool.
5. Beat the egg whites until they form stiff peaks. Sift in the flour, cocoa powder, confectioners' sugar, and Muscovado sugar. Mix the ingredients together carefully. Fold in the ground nuts and the butter, and beat to a smooth batter. Divide the batter evenly between the prepared cake pans.
6. Bake for about 35 minutes or until a toothpick inserted into the center comes out with moist crumbs.

MAKING THE CANDIED HAZELNUTS

1. Preheat the oven to 350°F.
2. Toast the hazelnuts on a pan in the oven for 12–15 minutes. Watch them carefully as they can burn quickly. If they aren't already skinned, rub them in a hand towel, loosening off as much of the skin as possible. Lay the nuts on a piece of baking parchment.
3. Heat the sugar in a saucepan until it begins to melt at the edges. Stir gently until all the sugar has dissolved and is golden brown. Pour the sugar over the nuts, and let them cool for 10 minutes.
4. Chop the candied nuts into small pieces.

MAKING THE CHOCOLATE FROSTING

1. Melt the chocolate in the top of a double boiler (see page 10) or in the microwave. Set the chocolate aside to cool to room temperature.

Continued on page 83 ⟫→

2. Beat the butter until light and fluffy. Gradually add the confectioners' sugar and cocoa powder and beat until the batter is smooth. Blend in the melted chocolate and the vanilla.
3. Add the coffee, 1 tablespoon at a time, and beat for a couple minutes until the frosting is smooth and shiny.

DECORATION
1. Press the pointed tip of a skewer into the side of each hazelnut.
2. Heat the sugar in a saucepan until melted and golden brown. Be careful—it will be very hot! Remove the pan from the heat, and allow the sugar to cool and thicken slightly. It will just take a few seconds—it's a quick job!
3. Spoon the melted sugar over a hazelnut, or drop the nut into the saucepan until the nut is covered. Hold the skewer over the pan so any extra sugar syrup can run off in a thin stream. Hold the skewer still until the stream begins to harden.
4. Place the skewer over the edge of the kitchen sink, holding it down with, for example, a heavy cutting board, until the sugar has completely hardened.
5. Carefully reheat the sugar, and repeat steps 3 and 4 until all the nuts have been coated with sugar.
6. Carefully remove the nuts from the skewers.

ASSEMBLING THE CAKE
1. Slice each layer in half horizontally so you will have four thin layers for the cake.
2. Place the first layer on a cake plate or board. Spread an even amount of Nougat Cream over the layer. Sprinkle some of the chopped candied nuts on top. Repeat until you've covered three layers. Place the last layer on top, cut side down.
3. Spread a thin layer of Chocolate Frosting all around the cake. Refrigerate the cake for about 20 minutes or until the frosting has set.
4. Add another layer of Chocolate Frosting, and use a spoon or spatula to add some texture to the frosting.
5. Decorate the cake with whole candied hazelnuts.

TRIPLE CHOCOLATE WITH MACARONS

This cake is ideal for true chocolate lovers! If you want to decorate it with macarons, make them a couple of days ahead and keep them in the refrigerator until the cake is ready. Don't be scared off by anyone who says that making macarons is difficult. They do go wrong sometimes—even for me—but when your baking session goes well, the totally perfect macarons are so satisfying!

8–10 SLICES

CHOCOLATE LAYERS
1 1/4 cups flour
6 tablespoons cocoa powder
1 cup granulated sugar
1 teaspoon baking powder
1 teaspoon baking soda
1/2 stick salted butter
2/3 cup buttermilk
6 tablespoons strong coffee
1 large egg

WHITE, DARK, AND MILK CHOCOLATE GANACHES
3 1/2 ounces white chocolate
3 1/2 ounces milk chocolate
7 ounces dark chocolate
    (70% cocoa)
1 1/4 cups whipping cream

DECORATIONS
chocolate sprinkles

CHOCOLATE FILLING
1 3/4 ounces dark chocolate
    (70% cocoa)
1/4 cup whipping cream

MAKING THE CHOCOLATE LAYERS

1. Preheat the oven to 350°F.
2. Prepare two 6-inch cake pans with butter and flour, crumbs, or parchment paper (see page 18). Alternatively, prepare one pan and bake in the same pan in two stages.
3. Sift the flour, cocoa powder, sugar, baking powder, and baking soda into a large bowl.
4. Melt the butter, and mix it in a separate bowl with the buttermilk and coffee.
5. Stir the butter mixture and the egg into the dry ingredients, and beat just until combined and the batter is smooth—do not overmix. Divide the batter evenly between the prepared cake pans.
6. Bake the layers in the center of the oven for about 30–35 minutes or until a toothpick inserted into the center comes out with moist crumbs.
7. Cool the layers for 10 minutes in the pans, and unmold them onto a wire cooling rack.

MAKING THE WHITE, DARK, AND MILK CHOCOLATE GANACHES

1. Chop each of the chocolates separately, and place each into its own bowl.
2. Heat the cream in a saucepan. Just before it reaches the boiling point, remove it from the heat immediately.
3. Divide the cream among the bowls of chocolate: use about two-thirds of the amount for the dark chocolate and divide the rest evenly for the white and milk chocolate. Wait 30 seconds, and stir each until the mixture is smooth and shiny. Cool the cream until it is easy to spread. If any of the ganache becomes too firm, carefully heat it for a few seconds at a time in the microwave.

Continued on next page ➣⟶

15-20 MACARONS

MERINGUE
whites from 2 medium eggs
$1^3/_4$ ounces blanched and peeled almonds (see box above)
$^3/_4$ cup confectioners' sugar
2 tablespoons granulated sugar
$^1/_2$ teaspoon vanilla
paste coloring or natural food coloring (optional)

ASSEMBLING THE CAKE

1. Slice each layer in half horizontally so you will have four thin layers for the cake.
2. Place the first layer on a cake plate or board. Spread an even amount of White Chocolate Ganache over the layer. If the ganache is too soft, refrigerate the cake for a few minutes before adding the next layer.
3. Add the next layer, and cover it with the Milk Chocolate Ganache.
4. Add the third layer, and cover it with some of the Dark Chocolate Ganache, making it the same thickness as the previous layers.
5. Place the last layer on top, cut side down. Cover the entire cake with a thin layer of Dark Chocolate Ganache to create a crumb coating. Refrigerate the cake for about 20 minutes or until the crumb coating has set.
6. Evenly spread the rest of the Dark Chocolate Ganache over the entire cake.
7. Before the ganache sets, decorate it with Macarons (recipe follows) set on their edges and chocolate sprinkles.

MACARONS

These cookies can be flavored with $^1/_4$ teaspoon vanilla powder (or vanilla extract) or 1 teaspoon grated lemon peel. You can also substitute about 5 percent of the confectioners' sugar with the same amount of cocoa powder.

MAKING THE MERINGUE

1. Prepare the egg whites a day in advance by placing them in a bowl covered with plastic wrap and allowing them to sit at room temperature.
2. Finely grind the almonds in a blender or food processor. Push them through a fine mesh. Mix the almonds with the confectioners' sugar, and grind the mixture to a very fine powder.
3. Beat the egg whites in a clean bowl using an electric or stand mixer. When the egg whites begin to foam, add the granulated sugar 1 tablespoon at a time. Continue beating until you have a thick, firm, and shiny meringue. Add the vanilla, and beat to incorporate. You should be able to tip the bowl without the meringue sliding out.

Continued on page 89 ⟫→

4. Use a rubber spatula to carefully fold the ground almonds into the meringue and add coloring at this point if desired. The meringue should be neither too soft nor too firm. You can test the consistency by dropping a bit of the meringue onto a piece of baking parchment. The drop should flatten out and develop a smooth surface after a few minutes. If it doesn't, stir the mixture a little more.
5. Fit a pastry bag with a round tip, and fill it with meringue. Press out small dollops onto a baking sheet covered with baking parchment. Keep in mind that the meringue will spread so don't make them larger than a quarter. Let the meringues rest for at least 1 hour on the pan so they can form a "skin" on the surface. Make sure the meringues aren't misshapen. If they won't set, leave them for a while longer in a warm place (such as on top of the oven as it heats up).
6. Preheat the oven to 325°F.
7. Bake the meringues for 11–13 minutes in the center of the oven. Keep an eye on them for the last few minutes. Move the baking sheet if the meringues start to brown. One way to test if the meringues are done is to lightly press the top of a cookie from one side. If the top gives, the meringue isn't done yet. You can also lightly push one meringue. If it loosens from the baking parchment, then it is ready.
8. Remove the meringues from the oven, and let them cool completely. Carefully lift the meringues from the parchment.

MAKING THE CHOCOLATE FILLING
1. Chop the chocolate, and place it in a bowl.
2. Heat the cream in a saucepan until it boilings.
3. Pour the cream over the chopped chocolate. Wait 30 seconds, and stir the mixture until it is smooth and shiny. Cool the filling until it is easy to spread.

ASSEMBLING THE MACARONS
1. Lay the meringues flat side up, and pipe out or drop the filling onto each.
2. Join the meringues in pairs to form the macarons.
3. Keep the macarons in an airtight jar in the refrigerator for 1–2 days before they will be eaten, or store them in the freezer for up to 2 weeks.

ORANGE AND DULCE DE LECHE CAKE

Dulce de leche is a caramel-like sauce from Latin America. You can buy ready-made dulce de leche in many countries (though I've never found it in Sweden!).

8–10 SLICES

ORANGE LAYERS

4 large eggs
$3/4$ cup flour
$1^1/_2$ teaspoons cornstarch
$1/2$ cup + $1/4$ cup granulated sugar, separated
$1^1/_2$ teaspoons baking powder
pinch of salt
4 tablespoons sunflower or canola oil
4 tablespoons freshly squeezed orange juice (juice from 1 orange)
1 tablespoon grated orange peel (from 1 navel orange)
1 teaspoon vanilla sugar

DULCE DE LECHE CREAM

$1^3/_4$ cups whipping cream
1 (14 oz) can dulce de leche

DECORATIONS

$1^3/_4$ ounces milk chocolate
6 tablespoons whipping cream

MAKING THE ORANGE LAYERS

1. Separate the egg whites and yolks into separate bowls (see page 12) so you have 4 whites and 3 yolks (save the extra yolk for something else). Allow them to come to room temperature.
2. Preheat the oven to 325°F.
3. Sift the flour, cornstarch, $1/2$ cup sugar, baking powder, and salt into a bowl.
4. Whisk the oil, egg yolks, orange juice, orange peel, and vanilla sugar in a separate bowl. Sift in the dry ingredients, and stir only until the batter holds together.
5. In a clean and dry bowl, beat the egg whites until they hold soft peaks. Add the remaining $1/4$ cup of sugar 1 tablespoon at a time, and continue beating the mixture to stiff peaks. You should be able to tip the bowl without the egg whites sliding out.
6. Carefully fold one-fourth of the egg whites into the batter to lighten it before adding the rest of the egg whites to preserve the air in the whites. Fold in another fourth of the egg whites. Mix just enough to eliminate any streaks of egg white. Repeat two more times with the remaining egg whites. Divide the batter evenly between two unbuttered 6-inch cake pans.
7. Bake the layers for 30–40 minutes or until the top is golden brown and a toothpick inserted in the center comes out with moist crumbs.
8. Take the pans out of the oven, and immediately turn them upside down onto a cooling rack to prevent the layers from collapsing at the center. The wire cooling rack allows air to flow all around the layers. Allow the layers to rest upside down in the pans until they are completely cooled. Then, take a knife and carefully loosen the cake around the sides of each pan. Hold each pan and shake gently to unmold the layers from the pans.

Continued on page 93 ⇒→

MAKING DULCE DE LECHE CREAM

1. In a separate bowl, whip the cream until stiff peaks form.
2. Fold the dulce de leche into the cream, and stir to a smooth cream. Use the cream immediately. (Store extra cream—and you will have plenty—in the refrigerator for 2–3 days.)

DECORATIONS

Chocolate Slivers

1. Heat the milk chocolate for a few seconds in the microwave. Do not let the chocolate melt—it just needs to soften.
2. Use a cheese slicer or potato peeler to shave chocolate slivers for the smooth sides of the cake.

Whipped Cream

1. In a clean and dry bowl, whip a small amount of cream until it is thick.

ASSEMBLING THE CAKE

1. Slice each layer in half horizontally so you will have four thin layers for the cake.
2. Place the first layer on a cake plate or board. Spread an even layer of Dulce de Leche Cream over the layer. Repeat until you've covered three layers. Place the last layer on top, cut side down.
3. Cover the entire cake with an even layer of Dulce de Leche Cream.
4. To decorate the cake, fit a pastry bag with a small star tip, and fill it with Whipped Cream. Pipe a pattern around the edge of the cake top.
5. Decorate the sides of the cake with the chocolate slivers.

BANANA CAKE WITH CARAMEL FROSTING

Caramel and banana is a wonderful flavor combination! This very moist cake reminds me of the especially good banana cake I ate as a child. Unfortunately that family recipe has disappeared, but this one is as close as I could come to the original.

8–10 SLICES

CARAMEL SAUCE
1 cup whipping cream
³/₄ cup granulated sugar
¹/₄ stick salted butter

BANANA LAYERS
³/₄ cup Muscovado sugar,
    loosely packed in measur-
    ing cup
³/₄ cup granulated sugar
³/₄ stick + 1 tablespoon salted
    butter, at room temperature
2 large eggs
2¹/₂ cups flour
1 teaspoon baking soda
2 large bananas
1 cup milk
¹/₄ cup Caramel Sauce

CARAMEL FROSTING
1¹/₄ sticks salted butter,
    at room temperature
7 ounces cream cheese or
    similar soft cheese
1¹/₂ cups confectioner's sugar
¹/₄ cup Caramel Sauce, or more
    depending on your taste

CARAMEL SHARDS
6 tablespoons sugar

MAKING THE CARAMEL SAUCE
1. Heat the cream slowly in a small saucepan.
2. Pour the sugar into another saucepan, and heat until lukewarm. Do not stir! When the sugar begins to melt and turn brown at the edges, carefully stir with a spoon in toward the center until all of the sugar has dissolved. Allow the saucepan to remain on the heat until the sugar is golden brown, but watch carefully because the sugar can burn quickly.
3. Slowly add the cream—watch to make sure it doesn't bubble over. Stirring carefully, add the butter, and stir a bit more. Allow the mixture to cool for a few minutes, and pour the sauce into a clean jar.

MAKING THE BANANA LAYERS
1. Preheat the oven to 325°F.
2. Prepare two 6-inch cake pans with butter and flour, crumbs, or parchment paper (see page 18). Alternatively, prepare one pan and bake in two stages.
3. Beat the Muscovado and granulated sugars with the butter until the mixture is light and fluffy. Add the eggs, and beat until the batter is light and fluffy.
4. In a separate bowl, mix the flour and baking soda together; then sift the dry ingredients into the batter.
5. Mash the bananas, and blend them with the milk. Stir and then beat the batter until it is smooth. Divide the batter evenly between the prepared cake pans. Pour ¹/₄ cup Caramel Sauce into each pan, and stir it in with a spoon.
6. Bake the layers for 60–65 minutes or until a toothpick inserted into the center comes out with moist crumbs.

MAKING THE CARAMEL FROSTING
1. Beat the butter until it is white. Add the cream cheese, and beat for a few more minutes.

Continued on next page ⟹→

2. Add the confectioners' sugar, and beat to an even and thick batter. Blend in the Caramel Sauce, and refrigerate the frosting for 15–20 minutes if it is too soft.

MAKING THE CARAMEL SHARDS

1. Melt the sugar in a saucepan over medium heat until it is golden brown.
2. Pour the melted sugar onto a baking sheet lined with baking parchment, and spread it out to a thin layer. Work quickly before the sugar hardens. Let it cool.
3. Break the hardened sugar into smaller pieces.

ASSEMBLING THE CAKE

1. Slice each layer in half horizontally so you will have four thin layers for the cake.
2. Place the first layer on a cake plate or board. Spread an even layer of Caramel Frosting over the layer. Repeat until you've covered three layers. Place the last layer on top, cut side down.
3. Cover the entire cake with a thin layer of Caramel Frosting. Refrigerate the cake for about 20 minutes so the frosting can set.
4. Set aside a small amount of the frosting for the decoration, and then spread the rest evenly over the entire cake. Fit a pastry bag with a small star tip, and fill it with frosting. Pipe rosettes around the top of the cake (see the photo on page 94).
5. Decorate the cake with Caramel Shards.

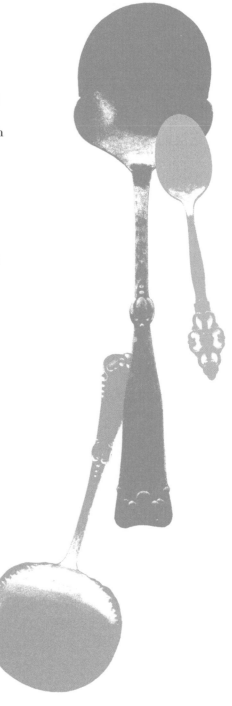

BLUEBERRY CAKE WITH LEMON BUTTERCREAM

A "groovy" cake filled with blueberries and tangy lemon buttercream. If possible, use fresh blueberries. Frozen blueberries will make the cake a little denser because the frozen berries contain more water.

12–15 SLICES

BLUEBERRY LAYERS
2 2/3 cups flour
2 teaspoons baking powder
2 tablespoons cornstarch
10 1/2 ounces blueberries
2/3 cup sour cream
3/8 cup milk
2 teaspoons vanilla sugar
2 teaspoons grated lemon peel
2 sticks salted butter,
    at room temperature
1 3/4 cups granulated sugar
4 large eggs

LEMON BUTTERCREAM
whites from 8 large eggs
2 cups granulated sugar
3 1/2 sticks unsalted butter,
    at room temperature
juice from 1/2 lemon
grated peel from 1 lemon
paste coloring or natural food
    coloring (optional)

MAKING THE BLUEBERRY LAYERS
1. Preheat the oven to 350°F.
2. Prepare three 8-inch cake pans with butter and flour, crumbs, or parchment paper (see page 18). Alternatively, prepare one pan and bake in several stages.
3. Sift the flour, baking powder, and cornstarch into a bowl. Blend 1 tablespoon of the flour mixture with the blueberries.
4. Blend the sour cream, milk, vanilla sugar, and grated lemon peel in a bowl.
5. Beat the butter and sugar until light and fluffy, and add the eggs one at a time. Beat well so each egg is incorporated into the batter before the next egg is added. Alternate adding small amounts of the flour and milk mixtures, and beat until the batter is smooth. Add the blueberries, and stir a few times so the berries are evenly distributed. Divide until the batter evenly among the prepared cake pans.
6. Bake the layers for 25–30 minutes or until a toothpick inserted into the center comes out with moist crumbs.

MAKING THE LEMON BUTTERCREAM
1. Pour the egg whites and sugar into a heatproof bowl, and set the bowl on top of a saucepan with some simmering water. Use a hand whisk to beat the mixture continually until it reaches 150°F or the sugar crystals have dissolved. Remove the bowl from the heat.
2. Beat the mixture with a hand or stand mixer until it is a white and fluffy meringue. Continue beating until the mixture is cool and thick. This step can take up to 10 minutes.
3. Add the butter a small amount at a time. After all the butter has been incorporated, continue beating for 3–5 minutes. (If your buttercream separates, see page 52.)

Continued on next page ➡→

Add the lemon juice and peel and, if desired, paste coloring or natural food coloring (see page 15).

ASSEMBLING THE CAKE

1. Place the first layer on a cake plate or board. Spread an even layer of Lemon Buttercream over the layer. Repeat for the next layer. Place the last layer on top, bottom side up for an even surface.

2. Cover the entire cake with a thin layer of Lemon Buttercream. Refrigerate the cake for about 20 minutes so the frosting can set.

3. Fit a pastry bag with a large round tip, and fill it with Lemon Buttercream. Press out three (or as many as you like) horizontal bands on the side of the cake. Begin at the base and work upward (see page 31).

4. Use an offset spatula slightly narrower than a band of buttercream to carefully expand the bands (see page 31). Continue the same way all around the cake and over the top.

SUMMER CAKE WITH STRAWBERRIES AND LIME

This cake is similar to classic shortcakes with whipped cream and strawberries between the layers. The fresh twist of lime adds a slight tang to the flavors.

8–10 SLICES

SUGAR CAKE LAYERS
$\frac{1}{2}$ stick salted butter
3 large eggs
1 cup granulated sugar
$\frac{1}{2}$ teaspoon vanilla powder
 or vanilla extract
6 tablespoons whole milk
$1\frac{1}{4}$ cups flour
$1\frac{1}{2}$ teaspoons baking powder

LIME CURD (ABOUT $1\frac{1}{4}$ CUPS)
$\frac{2}{3}$ cup granulated sugar
2 large eggs
juice and peel from 3 limes
 (about $\frac{1}{3}$ cup juice)
$\frac{1}{2}$ stick unsalted butter,
 cut into cubes

**WHIPPED CREAM FILLING
AND DECORATION**
$2\frac{1}{2}$ cups whipping cream
2 tablespoons sugar, or to taste
1 pound strawberries
6 tablespoons Lime Curd
 (see above)

MAKING THE SUGAR CAKE LAYERS
1. Preheat the oven to 350°F.
2. Prepare two 6-inch cake pans with butter and flour, crumbs, or parchment paper (see page 18).
3. Melt the butter, and let it cool.
4. Beat the eggs, sugar, and vanilla in a bowl until light and fluffy. Heat the milk, and add it gradually to the egg mixture. Beat in the butter.
5. Mix the flour and baking powder, and stir them into the batter. Divide the batter evenly between the prepared cake pans.
6. Bake the layers for about 30 minutes or until a toothpick inserted into the center comes out with moist crumbs.

MAKING THE LIME CURD
1. Pour the sugar, eggs, lime peel, and lime juice into a heatproof bowl, and place the bowl over a saucepan of simmering water. Use a hand whisk to beat the mixture continually. The curd should be as thick as hollandaise sauce.
2. Remove the curd from the heat, and stir in the butter until the mixture is smooth. Pour the curd into a lidded jar. It keeps for about 1 week in the refrigerator.

MAKING THE WHIPPED CREAM AND STRAWBERRIES
1. In a large bowl, whip the cream until it is thick. Add the sugar.
2. Rinse and slice the strawberries.

ASSEMBLING THE CAKE
1. Slice each layer in half horizontally so you will have four thin layers for the cake.
2. Place the first layer on a cake plate or board. Spread an even layer of Lime Curd over the layer, add a layer of whipped cream, and finish with sliced strawberries. Repeat until you've covered three layers. Place the last layer on top, cut side down.
3. Cover the entire cake with a thick layer of whipped cream, and decorate with strawberries.

LEMON LOVER'S DREAM CAKE

The super-fluffy layers of this cake are combined with one of my favorite fillings—lemon curd. It is the dream cake for lemon lovers. During baking, the layers puff up above the sides of the pan, but as soon as you remove them from the oven and flip them onto a cooling rack, they flatten.

8–10 SLICES

LEMON LAYERS
4 large eggs
$3/4$ cup flour
$1^1/2$ teaspoons cornstarch
$1/2$ cup + $1/4$ cup sugar
$1^1/2$ teaspoons baking powder
pinch salt
1 tablespoon lemon juice + 3
    tablespoons water
1 tablespoon grated lemon peel
1 teaspoon vanilla sugar

LEMON CURD (ABOUT $1^1/3$ CUPS)
$2/3$ cup granulated sugar
2 large eggs
juice and peel from 2 lemons
    (about 6 tablespoons lemon
    juice and 2 tablespoons peel)
$1/2$ stick unsalted butter, at room
    temperature, cut into cubes

LEMON CREAM (YIELD $1^3/4$ CUP)
$1^1/4$ cups whipping cream
2–3 tablespoons granulated sugar
6 tablespoons Lemon Curd
    (see above)

MAKING THE LEMON LAYERS

1. Separate the egg whites and yolks into separate bowls (see page 12) so you have 4 whites and 3 yolks (save the extra yolk for something else). Allow them to come to room temperature.
2. Preheat the oven to 325°F.
3. Sift the flour, cornstarch, $1/2$ cup sugar, the baking powder, and salt into a bowl.
4. Whisk the oil, egg yolks, lemon juice, lemon peel, and vanilla sugar in a separate bowl. Sift in the dry ingredients, and stir only until the batter holds together.
5. In a clean and dry bowl, beat the egg whites until they hold soft peaks. Add the remaining $1/4$ cup of sugar 1 tablespoon at a time, and continue beating the mixture to stiff peaks. You should be able to tip the bowl without the egg whites sliding out.
6. Carefully fold one-fourth of the egg whites into the batter to lighten it before adding the rest of the egg whites to preserve the air in the whites. Fold in another fourth of the egg whites. Mix just enough to eliminate any streaks of egg white. Repeat two more times with the remaining egg whites. Divide the batter evenly between two unbuttered 6-inch cake pans.
7. Bake the layers for 30–40 minutes or until the top is golden brown and a toothpick inserted in the center comes out with moist crumbs.
8. Take the pans out of the oven, and immediately turn them upside down onto a cooling rack to prevent the layers from collapsing at the center. The wire cooling rack allows air to flow all around the layers. Allow the layers to rest upside down in the pans until they have cooled completely. Then, take a knife and carefully loosen the cake around the sides of each pan. Hold each pan and shake gently to unmold the layers from the pans.

Continued on next page ➡→

MAKING THE LEMON CURD

1. Pour the sugar, egg, lemon peel, and lemon juice into a heatproof bowl, and place the bowl over a saucepan of simmering water. Use a hand whisk to beat the mixture continually so the curd doesn't harden and become scrambled eggs instead! The curd should be about the same thickness as hollandaise sauce.
2. Remove the curd from the heat and stir in the butter. Stir until the mixture is smooth. Pour it into a lidded jar. Lemon curd keeps for about 1 week in the refrigerator.

MAKING THE LEMON CREAM

1. Beat the cream and sugar together until incorporated.
2. Fold in the Lemon Curd to make a thick cream.

ASSEMBLING THE CAKE

1. Slice each layer in half horizontally so you will have four thin layers for the cake.
2. Place the first layer on a cake plate or board. Spread an even layer of Lemon Curd over the layer. Repeat until you've covered three layers. Place the last layer on top, cut side down.
3. Cover the entire cake with a layer of Lemon Cream.
4. Fit a pastry bag with a small star tip, and fill it with Lemon Cream. Pipe small rosettes all over the top of the cake. Decorate the cake with a few small pennants made with skewers and pretty ribbons.

DELUXE CARROT CAKE

Carrot cake with a cream cheese filling has become one of the classics. My version is an extra-deluxe variation with walnuts, cinnamon, and coconut. A cake that invokes autumn!

8–10 SLICES

CARROT CAKE LAYERS
$1^{1}/_{4}$ sticks salted butter
3 large eggs
$^{2}/_{3}$ cup white sugar
$^{2}/_{3}$ cup Muscovado sugar (firmly
    packed in measuring cup)
1 teaspoon vanilla sugar
$1^{1}/_{4}$ cups flour
2 teaspoons baking powder
$1^{1}/_{2}$ teaspoons baking soda
1 teaspoon cinnamon
$2^{1}/_{2}$ cups peeled and finely grated
    carrots
1 cup chopped walnuts
$^{2}/_{3}$ cup applesauce

CREAM CHEESE FROSTING
1 stick unsalted butter,
    at room temperature
$10^{1}/_{2}$ ounces cream cheese
    or a similar soft cheese
$1^{1}/_{2}$ cups confectioners' sugar
1 teaspoon vanilla sugar

DECORATION
$3^{1}/_{2}$ ounces (about $1^{1}/_{4}$ cups)
    coconut flakes
fabric flowers (optional)

MAKING THE CARROT CAKE LAYERS
1. Preheat the oven to 350°F.
2. Prepare two 6-inch cake pans with butter and flour, crumbs, or parchment paper (see page 18). Alternatively, prepare one pan and bake in two stages.
3. Melt the butter, and let it cool.
4. Beat the eggs with the granulated and Muscovado sugars until the mixture is light and fluffy. Mix in the butter and vanilla sugar, and beat a little more.
5. Blend the flour, baking powder, baking soda, and cinnamon, and sift it into the batter. Beat just until the batter holds together.
6. Fold the carrots, nuts, and applesauce into the batter. Divide the batter evenly between the prepared cake pans.
7. Bake the layers for 40–45 minutes or until a toothpick inserted into the center comes out with moist crumbs.

MAKING THE CREAM CHEESE FROSTING
1. Beat the butter until it is white. Add the cream cheese, and beat until the mixture is smooth and thick.
2. Add the confectioners' sugar and vanilla sugar, and beat a little more. If the frosting is not set enough, refrigerate it for a while.

ASSEMBLING THE CAKE
1. Slice each layer in half horizontally so you will have four thin layers for the cake.
2. Place the first layer on a cake plate or board. Spread an even layer of Cream Cheese Frosting over the layer. Repeat until you've covered three layers. Place the last layer on top, cut side down.
3. Spread the rest of the Cream Cheese Frosting over the whole cake, and sprinkle a layer of coconut flakes over the frosting. If necessary, lightly press the coconut into the frosting with your palm. Decorate the top with fabric flowers or any other decoration you like.

STRAWBERRY CAKE WITH WHITE CHOCOLATE

Here's a pretty cake that is sweet enough to easily satisfy any sweet tooth in one or two bites. Decorate the cake with fresh flowers—perhaps, as here, with beautiful roses. If you are lucky, you can pick the roses from your own garden. That would make this delicious dessert the ultimate summer cake.

12–15 SLICES

CAKE LAYERS
4 large eggs
1¹/₂ cups granulated sugar
1³/₄ cups flour
2¹/₂ teaspoons baking powder
2–4 ounces strawberries
¹/₄ cup water

STRAWBERRY COMPOTE

This tasty compote can be mixed with some whipped cream and, voilà, you have a wonderful strawberry mousse!

about 12 ounces strawberries
¹/₄ cup granulated sugar

WHITE CHOCOLATE FROSTING
7 ounces white chocolate
³/₄ stick + 1 tablespoon unsalted butter, at room temperature
7 ounces cream cheese, at room temperature
1–1¹/₄ cups confectioners' sugar
pink paste coloring or natural food coloring (optional)

DECORATION
fresh flowers, such as rose

MAKING THE CAKE LAYERS
1. Preheat the oven to 350°F.
2. Line an 8-inch cake pan with a high collar of baking parchment (see page 19).
3. Beat the eggs and sugar until light and fluffy, about 5 minutes.
4. Mix the flour and baking powder in a separate bowl.
5. Rinse and clean the strawberries. Blend the strawberries to a smooth purée. Stir the strawberry purée and water together, and heat the mixture in a saucepan until the mixture thickens.
6. Sift the flour, one-third at a time, into the egg mixture. Stir a few times after each sifting.
7. Stir in the strawberry purée, and slowly beat to a smooth batter. Pour the batter into the prepared cake pan.
8. Bake the cake for about 1 hour or until a toothpick inserted into the center comes out with moist crumbs. Let the cake cool completely in the pan.

MAKING THE STRAWBERRY COMPOTE
1. Rinse, clean, and slice the strawberries. Mix the strawberries and the sugar in a saucepan. Mash the strawberries to release a little water (or mash them completely if you like).
2. Boil the compote for about 30 seconds. Remove it from the heat, and let it cool.

MAKING THE WHITE CHOCOLATE FROSTING
1. Chop the chocolate into pieces, and melt the chocolate in a nonreactive heatproof bowl over a saucepan of simmering water. Allow the chocolate to cool.
2. Cream the butter and cream cheese.

Continued on page 113 ⇒→

3. In a separate bowl, blend the chocolate and confectioners' sugar to taste. Incorporate it with the butter and cream cheese.

4. If you like, color the frosting with paste coloring or natural food coloring (see page 15). Of course, the cake doesn't need to be pink. It will be just as pretty if it is white or any other color.

ASSEMBLING THE CAKE

1. Slice the cake in thirds horizontally so you will have three thin layers for the cake.

2. Place the first layer on a cake plate or board. Spread half of the Strawberry Compote over the cake. Repeat until you've covered two layers. Place the last layer on top, cut side down.

3. Spread a thin layer of White Chocolate Frosting over the whole cake. Refrigerate the cake for 20 minutes or until the frosting has set.

4. Cover the entire cake with a thick layer of White Chocolate Frosting.

5. Fit the pastry bag with a small round tip, and fill it with frosting. Pipe out small dots all around the base of the cake.

6. Decorate the cake with fresh flowers and perhaps a little pennant made with a skewer and some pretty paper.

RED VELVET CHEESECAKE

Red velvet is a favorite cake that I've baked many times. This version is very good—one of the tasty layers is a velvety lemon cheesecake, and the entire cake is covered with a whipped cream cheese frosting. Simply put—it's the best of three worlds. This is a good cake to make in several steps over a couple of days.

12–15 SLICES

RED VELVET LAYERS

1 cup whole milk

1 tablespoon white wine vinegar

1²/₃ cups flour

1 teaspoon baking soda

1 tablespoon cocoa powder

2 tablespoons cornstarch

1¹/₄ cups granulated sugar

2 large eggs

³/₄ cup sunflower or canola oil

2 tablespoons red caramel
coloring

CHEESECAKE LAYERS

21 ounces cream cheese

³/₄ cup granulated sugar

1 tablespoon juice and the grated
peel from 1 lemon

2 large eggs

²/₃ cup sour cream

1 tablespoon flour

CREAM CHEESE FROSTING

10¹/₂ ounces cream cheese

³/₄ cup confectioners' sugar

1¹/₄ cups whipping cream

MAKING THE RED VELVET LAYERS

1. Prepare two 8-inch cake pans with butter and flour, crumbs, or parchment paper (see page 18). Alternatively, prepare one pan and bake in two stages.

2. Mix the milk and vinegar in a bowl. Let the mixture stand 20–30 minutes until the mixture is room temperature and has thickened slightly. It will look as if it has separated.

3. Preheat the oven to 350°F.

4. Sift the flour, baking soda, cocoa powder, cornstarch, and sugar in a separate bowl.

5. Whisk the eggs, oil, milk mixture, and caramel coloring in a separate bowl, and stir in the dry ingredients. Beat for 1 minute, and divide the batter evenly between the prepared cake pans.

6. Bake the layers for 25–30 minutes or until a toothpick inserted into the center comes out with moist crumbs.

MAKING THE CHEESECAKE LAYERS

1. Preheat the oven to 325°F.

2. Line the bottom of a springform pan (the same size as the cake layers) with baking parchment. Boil the water to be used later for baking.

3. Cream the cream cheese, sugar, and lemon juice and peel. Add the eggs, and beat for 1 minute more. Blend in the sour cream, and sift in the flour. Stir to mix, and pour the batter into the prepared pan.

4. Place the springform pan in a roasting pan, and place the pan in the oven. Pour the boiling water into the roasting pan, filling it halfway up the springform pan. Bake for about 50 minutes or until the cheesecake is still slightly quivery but firm around the edges. Cool the cheesecake completely in the pan.

5. Cover the cheesecake and springform pan with plastic wrap, and freeze it for at least 2 hours. Freezing will

Continued on next page ⇒→

stabilize the cheesecake so it won't crumble when layered with the cake.

MAKING THE CREAM CHEESE FROSTING

1. Cream the cream cheese and confectioners' sugar in a bowl.
2. In a separate bowl, whip the cream until it is thick; fold it into the cream cheese mixture. If the frosting is clumpy, whip it until it is smooth, but be careful not to whip too much—that will make it runny! If the frosting is not firm enough, refrigerate it for a while.

ASSEMBLING THE CAKE

1. Take the cheesecake out of the freezer, but make sure it doesn't defrost completely.
2. Begin by placing a red velvet layer on a cake plate or board.
3. Remove the plastic wrap from the cheesecake, and release the rim and bottom of the springform pan. Place the cheesecake on top of the red velvet layer.
4. Top with the other red velvet layer, bottom side up. Cover the cake, and allow the cheesecake to thaw. As the cheesecake thaws, it will shrink in and push out at the sides. Use a knife held at a 90° angle to cut away any extra cheesecake around the cake.
5. Cover the entire cake with a thin layer of Cream Cheese Frosting to catch any crumbs. "Spackle" away any unevenness (see page 22). Refrigerate the cake for about 20 minutes.
6. Spread the rest of the frosting over the entire cake. Use a spoon to make a pattern in the frosting. Embellish the finished cake with a little paper heart fastened to a skewer or a drinking straw.

> ### CHANGING THE COLOR OF THE CAKE
>
> Not a fan of red velvet? The caramel coloring for the cake can be omitted or another color substituted.

PEACH MOUSSE CAKE WITH VANILLA

What could be more refreshing than a delicious combination of peaches and vanilla? The peach compote is so tempting that you will want to eat it right away. This cake has a very thick frosting—if you pipe on the frills. If you prefer a smoothly frosted cake, halve the meringue buttercream recipe.

8–10 SLICES

VANILLA LAYERS
1 stick salted butter,
    at room temperature
$1^3/_4$ cups granulated sugar
1 cup milk, at room temperature
$^1/_2$ teaspoon vanilla powder or
    extract (or $^1/_2$ vanilla bean)
$2^1/_4$ cups flour
1 teaspoon baking powder
whites from 2 large eggs

PEACH COMPOTE
You can also use store-bought peach jam instead of making compote from scratch.

$^1/_2$ pound peaches, sliced
3 tablespoons water
$^1/_2$ cup granulated sugar
$^1/_2$ teaspoon vanilla powder
    or vanilla extract

PEACH MOUSSE
1 cup whipping cream
6 tablespoons Turkish or Greek
    yogurt (10% milk fat)
1 recipe Peach Compote (see above)

MERINGUE BUTTERCREAM
whites from 8 large eggs
$1^3/_4$ cups granulated sugar
$3^1/_2$ sticks unsalted butter,
    at room temperature
4 teaspoons vanilla sugar
apricot paste coloring or natural
    food coloring

MAKING THE VANILLA LAYERS
1. Preheat the oven to 350°F.
2. Prepare two 6-inch cake pans with butter and flour, crumbs, or parchment paper (see page 18). Alternatively, prepare one pan and bake in two stages.
3. Beat the butter and sugar until light and fluffy, about 3–4 minutes. Add the milk and vanilla (or slice open a vanilla bean and scrape out and add the seeds). Beat until the batter is smooth. Set aside.
4. Measure the flour and baking powder in a small bowl, and add them to the butter mixture. Add the egg whites, and beat for 2 minutes.
5. Divide the batter evenly between the prepared cake pans.
6. Bake the layers for about 45 minutes or until a toothpick inserted into the center comes out with moist crumbs.

MAKING THE PEACH COMPOTE
1. Mix all the ingredients in a small saucepan. Bring the mixture to a boil, mashing the peaches slightly and stirring occasionally.
2. Simmer until the fruit is soft, about 10 minutes. Pour the compote into a clean bowl or lidded container; refrigerate the compote until it is cold.

MAKING THE PEACH MOUSSE
1. If there is any liquid in the peach compote, drain it away, reserving it to drizzle onto the cake layers.
2. In a separate bowl, whip the cream until it is firm.
3. Gently mix the yogurt and Peach Compote into the whipped cream.

Continued on page 120 ⇒→

MAKING THE MERINGUE BUTTERCREAM

1. Pour the egg whites and sugar into a heatproof bowl, and set the bowl on top of a saucepan of simmering water.
2. Use a hand whisk to beat the mixture continually until it reaches 150°F or the sugar crystals have dissolved. Remove the bowl from the heat. Beat the mixture with a hand or stand mixer until it is as fluffy and white as meringue. Continue beating until the mixture is cool and thick (the meringue won't slide out when you tilt the bowl). This can take 5–10 minutes.
3. Add the butter, a small amount at a time. After all the butter has been incorporated into the meringue, beat it for another 3–5 minutes. (If your buttercream separates, see page 52.)
4. Add the vanilla sugar and paste coloring or natural food coloring (see page 15).

ASSEMBLING THE CAKE

1. Slice each layer in half horizontally so you will have four thin layers for the cake.
2. Place the first layer on a cake plate or board. Drizzle the layer with the excess liquid from the Peach Compote. Spread an even layer of Peach Mousse over the layer. Repeat until you've covered three layers. Place the last layer on top, cut side down. If the cake seems unstable, refrigerate it for a few minutes before adding the next layer of frosting.
3. Cover the cake with a thin layer of Meringue Buttercream to even the surface and catch any crumbs (see page 22).
4. Spread on another thin layer of frosting so the cake is not visible through the frosting. Refrigerate the cake 20 minutes before piping on the ruffles.

PIPING RUFFLES

1. Fit a pastry bag with a small ruffle tip (see page 27). The larger the tip you use, the more frosting will be released.
2. Hold the pastry bag upright or so the tip lies smoothly against the cake plate. The small part of the tip should be turned away from the cake, and the thick part should be turned toward the cake. Keep the tip as close to the cake as possible so the ruffles will attach to the cake.
3. Begin at the base of the cake, and work upward while you move the pastry bag back and forth, from right to

left, to form the ruffles. You can make the ruffles as large or small as you like. Large ruffles will be more difficult to form.

4. Make the ruffles on top of the cake by angling the pastry bag a little more. Work from the outer edge in toward the center. You can also leave the top of the cake smooth.

5. Optional: Complete the decoration with a pretty flower, such as a peony.

APPLE CINNAMON CAKE WITH BROWNED BUTTER

This cake features an unusual frosting, one made with browned butter! The browned butter frosting gives the cake a delicate toffee flavor that goes so well with apples and cinnamon.

8–10 SLICES

APPLE AND CINNAMON LAYERS

$1^1/_4$ sticks salted butter
3 large eggs
$^2/_3$ cup granulated sugar
$^2/_3$ cup light Muscovado sugar, firmly packed in measuring cup
1 teaspoon vanilla sugar
$^1/_4$ teaspoon vanilla powder or vanilla extract
$1^1/_4$ cups flour
2 teaspoons baking powder
$1^1/_2$ teaspoons baking soda
$1^1/_2$–2 teaspoons cinnamon
$^2/_3$ cup applesauce
9 ounces grated apple (about 2 apples)

APPLE COMPOTE

$10^1/_2$ ounces peeled, seeded, and coarsely chopped apples (about $2^1/_2$ apples)
$^1/_3$ cup water
$^1/_4$ cup Muscovado sugar, firmly packed in measuring cup
$^1/_4$ teaspoon vanilla powder or vanilla extract

BROWNED BUTTER FROSTING

$1^3/_4$ sticks unsalted butter
1 cup confectioners' sugar
$^1/_3$ cup whipping cream
pinch of cinnamon (optional)

DECORATION

1 crabapple (or other tiny apple)

MAKING THE APPLE AND CINNAMON LAYERS

1. Preheat the oven to 350°F.
2. Prepare two 6-inch cake pans with butter and flour, crumbs, or parchment paper (see page 18). Alternatively, prepare one pan and bake in two stages.
3. Melt the butter, and let it cool.
4. Beat the eggs, sugars, and vanilla until the mixture is very light and fluffy. Mix in the butter, and beat a little more.
5. Mix the flour, baking powder, baking soda, and cinnamon in a separate bowl, and sift them into the egg mixture. Beat until the mixture is thoroughly blended.
6. Mix in the applesauce and grated apple, and beat until the batter is smooth. Divide the batter evenly between the prepared cake pans.
7. Bake 40–45 minutes or until a toothpick inserted into the center comes out with moist crumbs.

MAKING THE APPLE COMPOTE

1. Mix all the ingredients for the compote in a saucepan and simmer, uncovered, for 10–15 minutes or until the apples are soft.
2. Pour the mixture into a clean jar, and refrigerate.

Continued on page 125 ⇒→

MAKING THE BROWNED BUTTER FROSTING

Use only unsalted butter because otherwise the frosting will have grains of salt.

1. Melt the butter in a saucepan over low heat. Simmer while stirring constantly until the butter is a fine golden color. Stir until the butter stops sizzling and it smells toffee-like. If you want to remove the brown spots, pour the butter through a fine mesh sieve, coffee filter, or cheesecloth.
2. Pour the butter into a bowl, and let it cool for a while. Cover and refrigerate it until it starts to firm up.
3. Beat the butter until it is white. Add the confectioners' sugar, cream, and if desired, a pinch of cinnamon. Beat the mixture until it is fluffy.

ASSEMBLING THE CAKE

1. Slice each layer in half horizontally so you will have four thin layers for the cake.
2. Place the first layer on a cake plate or board. Spread on a layer of Apple Compote (you might also want to drizzle on some of the liquid from the compote). Repeat until you've covered three layers. Place the last layer on top, cut side down.
3. Place the cake on a cake turntable. Cover the cake with the Browned Butter Frosting, and use an offset spatula to form a pattern in the frosting. Begin on the top at the center of the cake, and hold the spatula down in the frosting so it will make a grooved pattern as you turn the cake. Use the same technique around the sides.
4. Garnish the cake with a crabapple or other tiny apple.

FROZEN TIRAMISÙ

This cake may look complicated, but it's actually a wonderfully tasty and easily made version of the classic tiramisù that I've been tempted by many times. If I had to choose, I'd say that the flavors in tiramisù are perfect! They just couldn't be any better. You can substitute the same amount of coffee or Marsala wine for the Kahlúa if you prefer.

10–12 SLICES

COOKIE BASE
3½ ounces plain butter cookies
  + 8–10 cookies for the middle
  (such as Marie cookies or
  tea biscuits)
½ stick unsalted melted
  and cooled butter

COFFEE SYRUP
2 tablespoons Kahlúa
3 tablespoons water
2 tablespoons instant coffee
  powder

MILK CHOCOLATE GANACHE
3½ ounces milk chocolate
⅓ cup whipping cream

MASCARPONE FILLING
6 tablespoons granulated sugar
2 egg yolks
3 large eggs
1 cup whipping cream
8 ounces mascarpone cheese
2 tablespoons Kahlúa

DECORATION
3½ ounces milk chocolate
  or dark chocolate
1–2 tablespoons cocoa powder

MAKING THE COOKIE BASE
1. Crush the cookies with a rolling pin, or grind them in the blender to fine crumbs.
2. Mix the cookies with the melted butter and form a dough. Line a springform (7–9½ inch diameter) with baking parchment between the bottom and release edge rim. Press the dough into the pan in an even layer. Place it in the freezer for 10 minutes.

MAKING THE COFFEE SYRUP
1. Pour the Kahlúa, water, and instant coffee powder into a saucepan, and simmer for about 5 minutes.
2. Remove it from the heat, and cool.

MAKING THE MILK CHOCOLATE GANACHE
1. Chop the chocolate, and place it in a bowl.
2. Heat the cream in a saucepan until just below the boiling point.
3. Pour the cream over the chocolate, wait 30 seconds, and stir to a shiny cream. Let the mixture cool slightly; the ganache should still be pourable.

MAKING THE MASCARPONE FILLING
1. Blend the sugar, egg yolks, and eggs in a large bowl. Place the bowl over a saucepan of simmering water. Beat the mixture with an electric beater until it has almost doubled in volume and is very fluffy and thick. Take it off the heat and let it cool slightly.
2. Whip the cream, mascarpone, and Kahlúa until the mixture thickens (but is still pourable). Add the egg mixture, and mix well.

ASSEMBLING THE CAKE
1. Take the springform pan out of the freezer, and pour about one-third of the Coffee Syrup evenly over the cookie base.

Continued on next page ⟹→

2. Pour half of the Chocolate Ganache onto the base, and place the springform pan in the freezer for 10 minutes (this step isn't absolutely necessary but it prevents the layers from blending into each other).

3. Pour half of the Mascarpone Filling onto the base. Dip the whole cookies in the Coffee Syrup and spread them evenly over the filling. Continue with the remainder of the Chocolate Ganache. Place it in the freezer again for 10 minutes to firm up (this step can be eliminated).

4. Pour on the rest of the Mascarpone Filling. Drizzle any leftover Coffee Syrup over the cake. Cover the Tiramisù, and freeze it for 6–8 hours.

DECORATION

1. Take the cake out of the freezer about 30 minutes before serving.

2. Very carefully soften the chocolate in the microwave—it shouldn't melt. Shave slivers of chocolate, using a cheese slicer on the smooth surface of the chocolate.

3. Sift cocoa powder over the cake, and decorate the cake with the chocolate slivers immediately before serving.

NO BAKE CHEESECAKE

Here's a super-easy and extra-tasty cake with a frozen chocolate base topped with a wonderful creamy vanilla cheesecake! It's the perfect cake to make on a warm summer day when you don't want to turn on the oven. Take the cake out of the freezer about half an hour before serving so it can thaw slightly.

10–12 SLICES

**CHOCOLATE SANDWICH
COOKIE BASE**
20 chocolate sandwich cookies
$1/2$ stick melted unsalted butter

CHEESECAKE FILLING
10 ounces cream cheese, softened
8 ounces ricotta cheese
$3/4$ cup granulated sugar
$1\,1/4$ cups whipping cream
2 teaspoons vanilla sugar

DECORATION
$1\,3/4$ ounces dark chocolate
fresh berries, such as strawberries
confectioners' sugar to sift over
    the cake (optional)

MAKING THE CHOCOLATE SANDWICH COOKIE BASE
1. Crush the cookies with a rolling pin, or grind them in the blender to fine crumbs. Mix the cookies with the melted butter.
2. Line a springform (7–$9\,1/2$-inch diameter) with baking parchment between the bottom and the release edge rim. Press the dough into the pan in an even layer. If the pan is 7 inches in diameter, then the cookie base will be at least $2\,3/4$ inches high. Refrigerate for 20 minutes.

MAKING THE CHEESECAKE FILLING
1. Beat the cream cheese, ricotta, granulated sugar, cream, and vanilla sugar together in a stand mixer (or hand blender) until the filling is thick but still pourable.
2. Pour the filling over the cookie base.

DECORATION
1. Break the chocolate into pieces, and melt it in a saucepan or the microwave. Cool slightly.
2. Drizzle the chocolate over the cheesecake. Use a spoon to spread the chocolate carefully and evenly over the cake in a pretty pattern. Cover the cake with plastic wrap, and freeze it for 6–8 hours.
3. Remove the cake from the freezer about 30 minutes before serving. Decorate it with your favorite berries, and if you like, sift a little confectioners' sugar over the fruit.

FROZEN MANGO PASSION

A wonderfully fresh and tart cake with exotic flavors that are just a bit different. It's also really easy to make. You can buy frozen mango pieces, but I think you should make the effort to find a fresh, perfectly ripe mango.

10–12 SLICES

GRAHAM CRACKER BASE
10 graham crackers
$1/2$ stick melted unsalted butter

CHEESECAKE FILLING
$10 1/2$ ounces cream cheese
$8 3/4$ ounces ricotta cheese
$1 3/4$ cups whipping cream
$3/4$ cup granulated sugar
1 teaspoon grated lemon peel
1 cup diced mango

DECORATION
3 passion fruits

MAKING THE GRAHAM CRACKER BASE
1. Grind the graham crackers to fine crumbs.
2. Mix the cracker crumbs with the melted butter, and press the mixture into the bottom of a 7–$9 1/2$-inch springform pan. Refrigerate for 20 minutes.

MAKING THE CHEESECAKE FILLING
1. Whisk the cream cheese, ricotta, cream, sugar, and lemon peel together until the filling is thick but still pourable. Pour the filling over the graham cracker base.
2. Blend the mango to a purée. Drizzle the purée over the filling, and stir it with a spoon until the purée is evenly distributed in the mixture.
3. Cover the cheesecake with plastic wrap, and freeze for 6 hours.

DECORATION
1. Remove the cheesecake from the freezer about 30 minutes before serving.
2. Cut up the passion fruits, and sprinkle them evenly over the cake.

FRILLY CAKE

Follow this basic recipe for a layer cake, then cover it with fondant and add the frills. Feel free to cover the cake with fresh berries, jam, or whatever you like. The meringue buttercream can be enhanced with fruit purée or melted chocolate. The cake looks big in the photo, but it is actually a mini layer cake. You can make a professional-looking layer cake even if you are not serving very many!

10–12 SLICES

CHOCOLATE LAYERS
$1/2$ stick + 1 tablespoon salted butter
$1^3/_4$ cups + 2 tablespoons flour
$2/_3$ cup cocoa powder
$1^1/_2$ teaspoons baking powder
$1^1/_2$ teaspoons baking soda
$1^2/_3$ cups granulated sugar
$3/_4$ cup + 2 tablespoons milk
2 medium eggs
$2/_3$ cup boiling water

MERINGUE BUTTERCREAM
The amount of buttercream below should be enough to fill and cover both the small and large cakes.

whites from 8 large eggs
$1^3/_4$ cups granulated sugar
$3^1/_2$ sticks unsalted butter, at room temperature
4 teaspoons vanilla sugar

FRILLS
$10^1/_2$–14 ounces fondant or flower paste (the flower paste will harden)

MAKING THE CHOCOLATE LAYERS
1. Preheat the oven to 350°F.
2. Prepare two 6-inch cake pans and one rectangular pan about 11 × 8 inches with butter and flour, crumbs, or parchment paper (see page 18).
3. Melt the butter, and allow it to cool.
4. Sift the flour, cocoa powder, baking powder, and baking soda into a large bowl. Add the sugar, milk, eggs, and boiling water, and beat for a couple of minutes to a smooth batter. Divide the batter evenly among the prepared cake pans.
5. Bake the round layers for 30–35 minutes and the rectangular one for about 20 minutes. The cakes are done when a toothpick inserted into the center comes out with moist crumbs.
6. Cool the layers in their pans. Unmold the two round layers from the pans, and let them continue to cool. Cut three circles, each $3^1/_2$ inches in diameter, from the rectangular layer using a cookie cutter (see page 10).

MAKING THE MERINGUE BUTTERCREAM
1. Pour the egg whites and sugar into a heatproof bowl. Place the bowl over a saucepan of simmering water. Use a hand whisk to beat the mixture continually until it reaches 150°F or the sugar crystals have dissolved. Remove the bowl from the heat. Beat the mixture with a hand or stand mixer until it is as fluffy and white as meringue. Continue beating until the mixture is cool and thick. This can take up to 10 minutes.
2. Add the butter a small amount at a time. When all the butter has been incorporated, beat for another 3–5 minutes. Add the vanilla sugar. (If your buttercream separates, see page 52.)

Continued on page 139 ⟫→

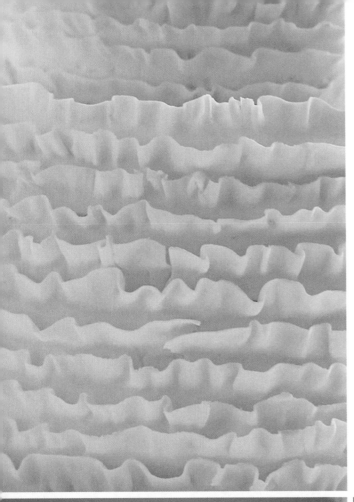

CAKE TIPS

You will need about 1 pound of fondant to cover the small cake. To cover cakes with fondant, see page 24. To stack the layers, see page 28.

   Refrigerate the small layers while you fill the large ones. Cold layers are easier to work with, and they crumble less when they are cold.

ASSEMBLING THE LARGE CAKE

1. Slice each large (6-inch diameter) layer in half horizontally so you will have four thin layers for the cake. Place the first layer on a cake plate or board. Spread an even layer of Meringue Buttercream over the layer. Repeat until you have covered three of the layers. Place the last layer on top, cut side down.
2. Cover the entire cake with a thin layer of Meringue Buttercream to contain the crumbs (see page 22). Refrigerate the cake for about 20 minutes.
3. Add another layer of Meringue Buttercream to even out the surface of the cake. Cover the cake with fondant (see page 24).

ASSEMBLING THE SMALL CAKE

1. Place the first small layer on a cake board, and cover it with an even layer of Meringue Buttercream. Repeat until you have three layers covered. Place the last layer on top, bottom side up.
2. Cover the entire cake with a thin layer of Meringue Buttercream. Refrigerate for about 20 minutes.
3. Add another layer of Meringue Buttercream to even out the surface of the cake. Cover the cake with fondant (see page 24).

STACKING THE CAKE

Follow the instructions on page 28 to stack the cake.

MAKING THE FRILLS

1. Begin by kneading a small amount of fondant or flower paste. If you work with only a small amount at a time, it won't dry out. Knead in a little confectioners' sugar if the fondant is too messy.
2. Sprinkle the work surface with confectioners' sugar. Roll out the fondant very thin. Cut it into strips with a pizza cutter. The narrower the strips are, the narrower the frills will be, and vice versa.
3. Use the shaft of a paint brush or something similar to form the frills. Carefully press down with the shaft and roll it back and forth over the strip to shape the ruffles.
4. Drizzle a little edible glue (you can purchase this at specialty shops on the Internet; see page 10) or water on the side of the strip that will be attached to the cake. Carefully attach the first strip at the top of the cake side so that the frill sticks up just over the edge.

Continued on next page ➡→

Continue the same way all around the cake until the first tier is complete. Begin tier 2 as you began tier 1, and continue attaching the tiers of frills until the entire cake is covered.

MAKING THE FLOWERS

1. Knead and color a small amount of fondant or flower paste (flower paste is recommended because it hardens more quickly) with your choice of color.
2. Sprinkle the work surface with confectioners' sugar. Use a rolling pin to roll out the paste in a thin layer. Use a round cookie cutter in any size (see page 10) to cut out the circles. The larger the cookie cutter is, the larger the flowers will be, and vice versa.
3. Make the ruffles around the edges of the circles by carefully rolling the shaft of a paint brush back and forth. Fold or press the flowers together from the center so that the edges overlap irregularly.
4. Let the flowers dry before you place them on the cake.

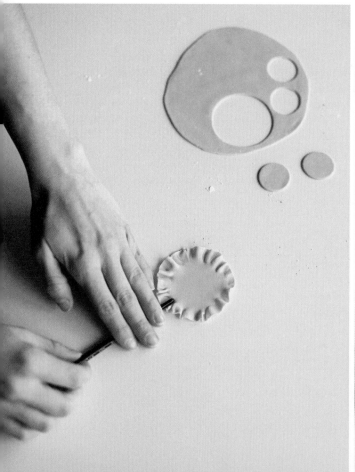

INDEX

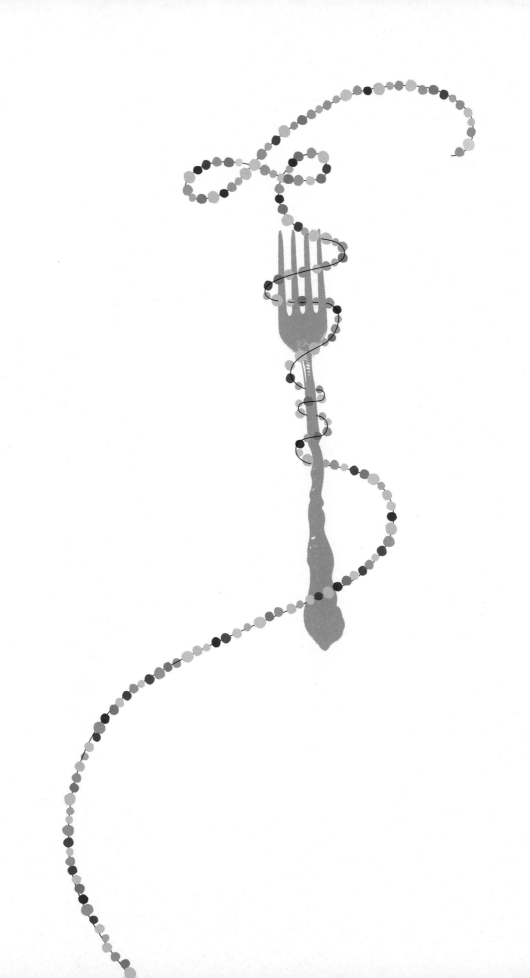

ACKNOWLEDGMENTS

A big thank you to . . .

. . . Lisa Ydring, my publisher, who believed absolutely in this book project.

. . . Anna Paljak, my editor, for her knowledge and patience.

. . . Katy Kimbell, for the lovely design!

. . . Christian, because you withstood many sleepless nights, cake tastings, and a mountain of dishes!

. . . My family and friends, because you always offered help and didn't complain that I never call!

. . . Emma, because you always tell it like it is and you never say no to a piece of cake!

. . . Elvira Antiques & Curiosities in Halmstad, Sweden, for so graciously lending me so many pretty things!

Roost Books
An imprint of Shambhala Publications, Inc.
Horticultural Hall
300 Massachusetts Avenue
Boston, Massachusetts 02115
roostbooks.com

Original text and photos ©2012 Linda Lomelino
English translation ©2014 Shambhala Publications, Inc.

First published by Bonnier Fakta, Stockholm, Sweden
Published in the English language by arrangement with Bonnier Group Agency, Stockholm, Sweden
Translated into English by Carol Huebscher Rhoades

Graphic design: Katy Kimbell
Illustrations: Katy Kimbell
Editor: Anna Paljak
Reproduction: Bop Punkthuset, Göteborg

9 8 7 6 5 4 3 2 1

First Edition
Printed in China

♺ This edition is printed on acid-free paper that meets the
American National Standards Institute Z39.48 Standard.
♻ Shambhala Publications makes every effort to print on recycled paper.
For more information please visit www.shambhala.com.

Distributed in the United States by Penguin Random House LLC
and in Canada by Random House of Canada Ltd

Library of Congress Cataloging-in-Publication Data

Lomelino, Linda.
[Lomelinos tårtor. English]
Lomelino's cakes: 27 pretty cakes to make any day special / Linda Lomelino;
translated by Carol Huebscher Rhoades.
Pages   cm
Includes index.
ISBN 978-1-61180-150-7 (alk. paper)
1. Cake. I. Title.
TX771.L6613 2014
641.86'53—dc23
2013042187